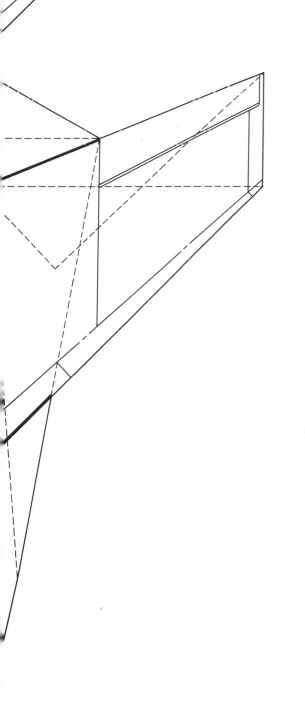

Flying Origami

Origami
from Pure Fun
to True Science

by Eiji Nakamura

 JAPAN PUBLICATIONS, INC.

Contents

Published by JAPAN PUBLICATIONS, INC., Tokyo and New York

Distributors:
UNITED STATES: *Kodansha International/USA, Ltd., through Harper & Row, Publishers, Inc.,*
10 East 53rd Street, New York, New York 10022. SOUTH AMERICA: *Harper & Row, Publishers*
Inc., International Department. CANADA: *Fitzhenry & Whiteside Ltd., 195 Allstate Parkway,*
Markham, Ontario L3R 4T8. MEXICO AND CENTRAL AMERICA: *HARLA S. A. de C. V.,*
Apartado 30–546, Mexico 4, D. F. BRITISH ISLES: *International Book Distributors Ltd., 66*
Wood Lane End, Hemel Hempstead, Herts HP2 4RG. EUROPEAN CONTINENT: *Fleetbooks,*
S. A., c/o Feffer and Simons (Nederland) 61 Strijkviertel, 3454 PK de Meern, The Netherlands.
AUSTRALIA AND NEW ZEALAND: *Bookwise International, 1 Jeanes Street, Beverley, South*
Australia 5007. THE FAR EAST AND JAPAN: *Japan Publications Trading Co., Ltd., 1–2–1,*
Sarugaku-cho, Chiyoda-ku, Tokyo 101.
© 1972 by Eiji Nakamura. LCCC No. 70–188761, ISBN 0–87040–023–1, First edition published
in May 1972, Twelfth printing in November 1986, Printed in U.S.A.

Preface

My fondness for the many arresting shapes possible with the simple techniques
of origami dates to my childhood. When I was only four years old, my mother
made an origami crane for me, and the wonder of its production and charm
of its appearance have never left me. Fifty years later, in 1968, I was still
devoted to origami, but I was also preoccupied with a long-cherished dream: an
aircraft that can fly by means of human power alone. I had, in fact, made an
experimental craft twenty feet long with a wingspread of sixty-nine feet.
One day, as I was on my way to the airport for further tests of my plane, a
reckless truck driver ran into my automobile injuring me to the extent that I was
forced to spend two months in the hospital.

But this was not a total misfortune, for while I was hospitalized I had a chance
to do a great deal of thinking and studying about origami aircraft. A very trifling
incident led me to attempt origami aircraft that resemble the real planes more
closely than old-fashiond versions. One day as I was folding paper planes for
some children, a young boy examined a plane I had made and then asked why
origami planes lack vertical tail sections (vertical stabilizers) like those of real
aircraft. I was a little surprised because, although I had never thought about it,
origami airplanes of the old kinds never had vertical stabilizers—though some of
them had vertically descending tails. I decided then that I would try to make
origami models that not only were more like real planes in appearance but also
that would perform better.

I soon learned however that traditional square origami paper is insufficient to
my purposes. After trying rectangular papers of various length-heighth
proportions, I finally discovered that a rectangle with proportions of $1 : \sqrt{2}$
permitted clean and efficient treatment of joints and corners yet resulted in little
waste.

Not only is it rational and convenient from the origami standpoint, but this
rectangle also teaches a number of facts and laws about the general treatment
of geometric figures. Because it contains many regular geometric figures within
itself, I have called this rectangle the true-rectangle, and I have spent a great
deal of time studying it. This book is the first tangible product of my research
into the nature of the true-rectangle. It is my hope that you will enjoy delving
into the possibilities of this figure as much—if not more—than making the
origami figures introduced here.

The fact that origami based on the true-rectangle are beautiful and easy to
make seems to me to illustrate the principle that there is no waste in truth, in
itself the most important theme of all scientific pursuits. I have used the word
"science" in the title of this book because origami based on the true-rectangle
are one part of truth.

As a last piece of advice I might say that perfection of any one of the origami
in this book requires application and care plus the perseverance to make a single
model several times until it is correct in all parts. But during the process you
are certain to learn important things that will be of value.

Tokyo, 1972

Eiji Nakamura

Origami from Pure Fun to True Science

1. THE LESSON OF THE MOON FLOWER

In Japan we raise annual plants called moon flowers that resemble morning glories in most respects except that they bloom in the evening instead of the morning. I am especially fond of these flowers and invariably have a number of pots of them to enjoy on summer evenings.

Once as I was looking at a particular blossom, I noticed something for the first time. On each petal, near the outer edge there is a long narrow triangle, intersecting the radial lines running from the center of the flower and composed of one convex fold and two concave folds. Turning to another flower I saw that in it, the triangular folds were about to open. Obviously without folding of this kind, the large petals of the moon flowers could not possibly be contained within their small buds. In contrast to the clarity and perfection of the triangle in unblemished flowers, those in half-open or distorted blooms were invariably irregular. This seemed to reveal the same simple, clear beauty possible in ideal origami and at the same time to demonstrate the strict natural law that turning one's back on providence is unrewarding.

In the world of nature there is no waste; truth knows no contradictions or limitations. Once I had humbly acknowledged this fact, I turned again to nature in my pursuit of truth. In short, the lovely moon flower taught me the unlimited possibilities inherent in origami and the truth they conceal. It also leads me to invite you my reader to share in developing the origami world of fantasy.

2. WHAT IS THE TRUE-RECTANGLE?

Before moving to the origami aircraft themselves I must briefly explain the nature of the true-rectangle. First it is a four-sided, regular figure with a side ratio of $1 : \sqrt{2}$. Since its characteristics teach useful things about the creation and production of many other origami as well as flying ones, the reader ought to understand them thoroughly.

A. The long side of the true-rectangle is equal in length to the diagonal of a square all of whose sides are as long as the short side of the true-rectangle.

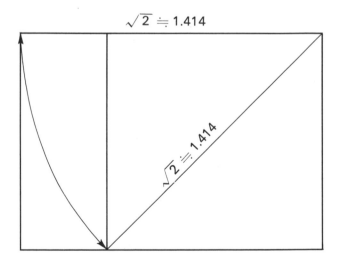

$$\sqrt{2} \fallingdotseq 1.414$$

B. A perpendicular bisecting the long sides of a true rectangle produces two true-rectangles. Furthermore doubling the short sides of a true-rectangle produces two true-rectangles. This means that the figure is boundless in the directions of both its long and short sides.

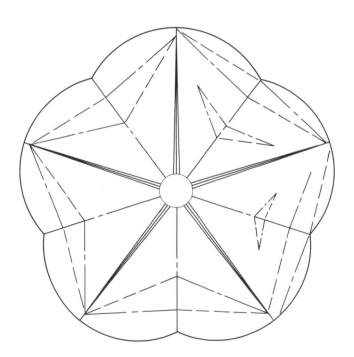

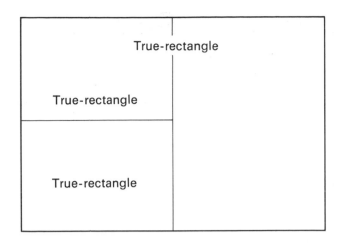

C. By removing a square all of whose sides are equal to the short side of a true-rectangle from that true-rectangle and repeating this process from the remaining rectangle (not a true-rectangle) it is possible to produce a small true-rectangle.

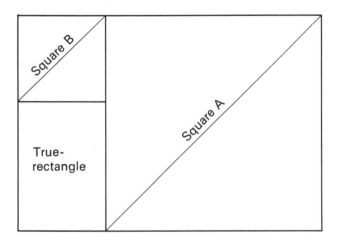

3. POSSIBILITIES OF THE TRUE-RECTANGLE

Aside from the characteristics described in the preceding section, the true-rectangle has a number of other important possibilities. For instance, unlike other figures, it will reveal lines by which a right angle may be divided into any number of equal parts.

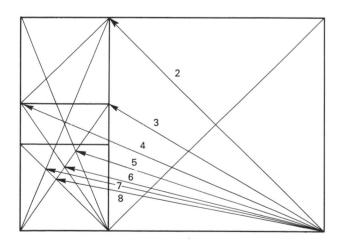

(The figures indicate the number of equal parts into which the right angle in the lower right corner is divided: 2 means it has been bisected, 3 that is has been trisected, etc.)

In addition, it will help one find correct side lengths for equilateral triangles, regular hexagons, and other regular polygons.

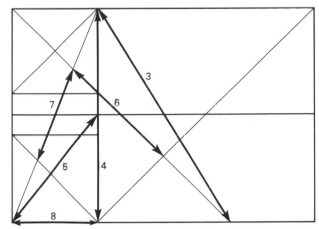

(The figures indicate maximum side lengths of regular polygons that may be produced from this true-rectangle.)

It will also give the radii of circles that will circumscribe these figures.

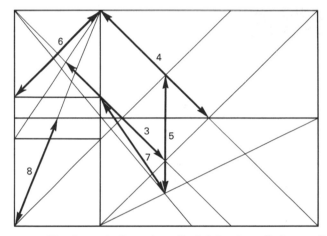

(The figures indicate the radii of circles that will circumscribe the regular polygons described above.)

From the origami viewpoint this is of the greatest importance since it makes it possible to fold accurate triangles, quadrilaterals, and many other polygons. This great advantage becomes clear when one recalls how troublesome it is to fold a pentagon with traditional square origami paper.

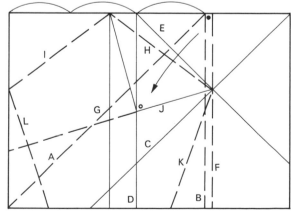

(Folds must be made in alphabetical order.)

But this figure contains many other fascinating possibilities which you will discover as you examine it and practice folding pieces of paper cut to its proportions.

Preparing to Begin

1. TOOLS AND MATERIALS

Making flying origami requires nothing that is not ordinarily found in the home. You will need plenty of paper, some glue (preferably plastic-base glue), scissors (or a paper cutter), stapler, and ruler. Because this book requires paper cut to the true-rectangle, however, I must explain how to produce it. It is not commercially available in many countries; therefore, the reader will have to cut the paper on hand to the correct proportions. Incidentally, when I began writing this book true-rectangle paper was on sale in Japan, and the observant reader may already have noticed that this book itself is made to those proportions.

Using characteristic (A) of this figure described on page 4 one can make true-rectangle paper with a compass. First, using the compass, measure the short side of an ordinary piece of rectangular paper. Transpose this length to the long side of the same piece. Erect a perpendicular at this point, and you will have produced a square whose sides are equal in length to the short side. You can find the length of the long side of the true-rectangle based on this short side by measuring the diagonal of the square with the compass.

If you make the original true-rectangle from a fairly large piece of paper you can easily make small true-rectangles by folding the large one in half as many times as is necessary. For the purposes of this book it is easier to prepare a piece of paper 210 by 148 mm (about $8\frac{1}{4}$ by $5\frac{3}{4}$ in.) and trace it as needed for all of the models use paper that size. For certain parts of models, however, smaller paper is needed. In such cases the paper size is referred to by a letter and a number—for instance B7. The sizes represented in this way are listed on the back of the cover. Finally, use the following method to verify the accuracy of the true-rectangle paper you have made.

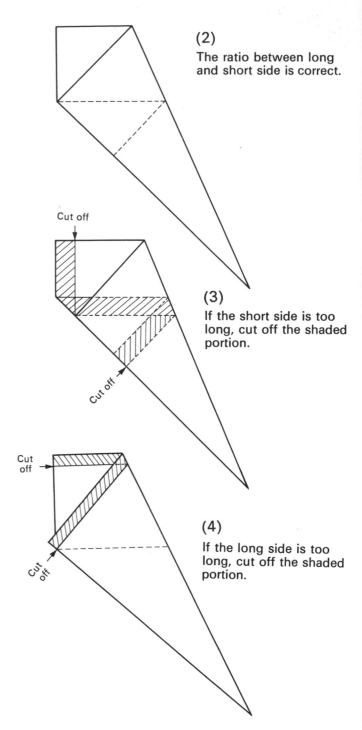

(2)
The ratio between long and short side is correct.

Cut off

(3)
If the short side is too long, cut off the shaded portion.

Cut off

Cut off

Cut off

(4)
If the long side is too long, cut off the shaded portion.

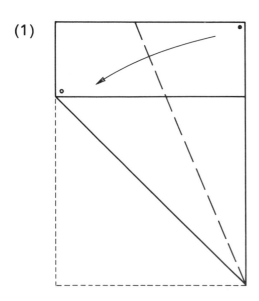

(1)

2. BRIEF NOTES ON TECHNIQUES

1. All folds must be perfectly straight. Make ample use of a ruler or your fingernails to achieve this.
2. Your hands must be clean and dry to prevent the paper's warping.
3. Right and left sides of all models must be symmetrical. Since aircraft must ordinarily maintain this symmetry, all models in this book—except where specifically stated otherwise—must follow this rule.
4. Always have the perseverance to fold and refold even when your are not sure you understand the model and be determined to make your models as good as you can.

3. SYMBOLS AND FOLDING TECHNIQUES

Symbol	Meaning	Result
	—— — —— — —— = valley fold (broken line) —— — — —— = peak fold (line of long and short dashes) ⌒⟶ = fold forward (or to you) ⌒⟶ = fold under (or away from you)	
	- - - - - - - - - (dotted line) = line already concealed, line to be folded in a coming step, or outline of the former position of a part •⟶∘ = bring the black dot to the white dot ⟵⟶ ⌐Cut = make a cut as long as the line shown	
	pocket fold; the paper is pressed inward so that the upper right corner falls inside the fold at a position approximately where the arrowhead is located = insert the flap	
Turn over	= make these folds in series beginning at the top = fold to form a right angle Turn over ⟶ = turn the entire figure over	
A B B	⌒⟶ = align the two heavy lines ⌐A ⌐B = perform the operations in alphabetical order; in this case first peak fold on line A then valley fold on line B	 ◕ = center of gravity

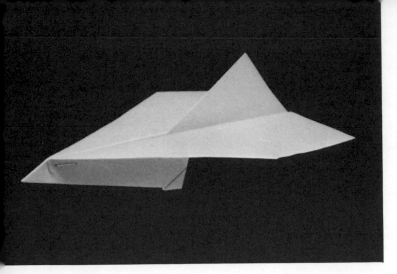

Planes for the Fancy

1. ARROWHEAD CRAFT

This new version of an old paper model has an added rising vertical stabilizer. Please note the small triangular folded section because it holds the forward section of the model firmly in place. Do not point the nose too sharply; for the sake of safety about 5′ is a good angle.

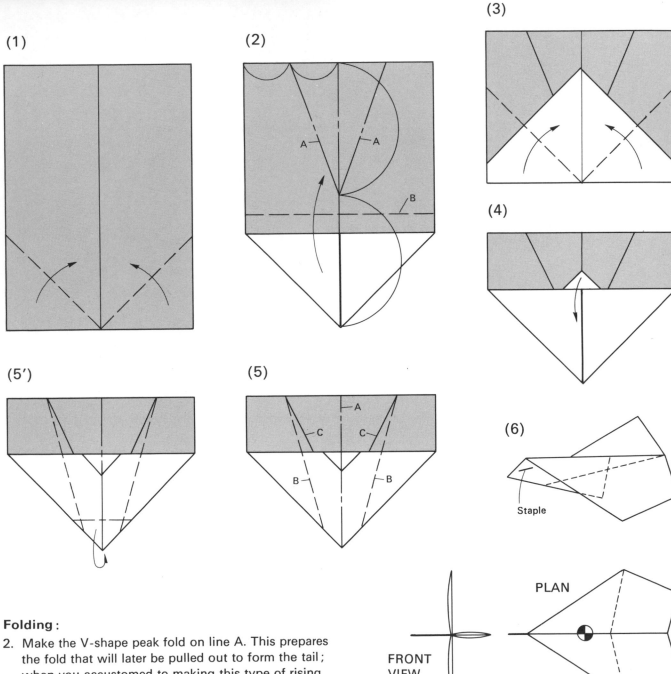

(1)

(2)

(3)

(4)

(5′)

(5)

(6)

Staple

Folding:

2. Make the V-shape peak fold on line A. This prepares the fold that will later be pulled out to form the tail; when you accustomed to making this type of rising stabilizer, you may omit this step. Next make a valley fold on line B.

5–6. Fold the entire fuselage in half on center line A and fold both wings downward on lines B. Now pull out the tail section (lines C) that you prepared in step 2. Staple the nose section as shown. At this point you may fold the nose downward (5′).

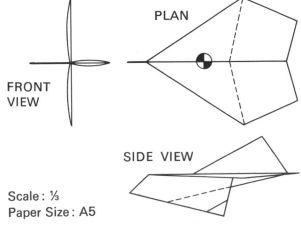

PLAN

FRONT VIEW

SIDE VIEW

Scale : ⅓
Paper Size : A5

2. ARROW-FEATHER CRAFT

Folding true-rectangular paper on a diagonal or a slanting line near a diagonal results in imperfect overlapping so that in places the underside of the paper is exposed. Though at first this seems difficult to handle, on further investigation it turns out to be one more of the limitless possibilities of this figure. By paying no attention to the imperfect overlap and continuing to fold, a number of variant forms may be produced. This craft is a variation created as a result of asymmerty. Modifications of it appear later in the book.

(1)

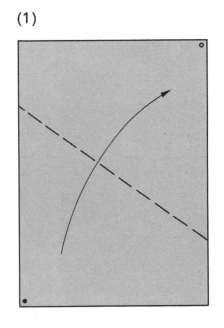

(2)

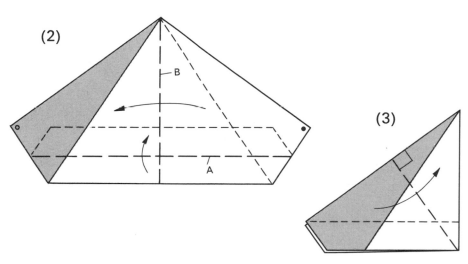

(3)

3. Bring the top layer only of the left lower side of the figure upward to the right by valley folding on the broken line.

(5)

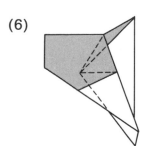

A (Staple)

(4)

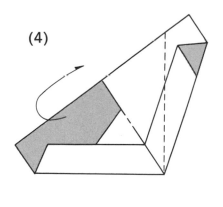

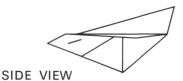

SIDE VIEW

(6)

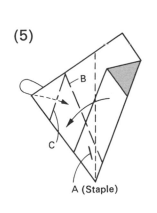

FRONT VIEW

PLAN

Scale : ⅓
Paper Size : A5

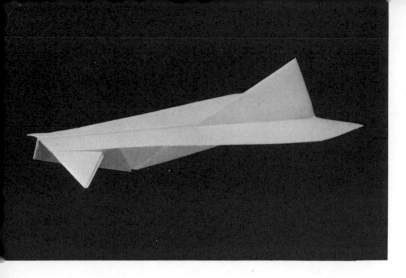

3. SQUID CRAFT

Although the squid has long been a favorite—under the name of the forward-wing or Canard—it tends to roll because the wingspan is too short fot the length of the body. A modification of the basic plane to remedy this fault appears later. The squid simply adds a rising vertical tail section to modernize the old plane a bit.

Because of their vital importance to the proper functioning of the craft, never make creases in the upper surfaces of flying origami planes or origami birds. To be even more strict, I might add that it is a bad idea to allow the underside of paper to become the upper surface of wings. From both the artistic and the scientific aerodynamic viewpoints it is always best to conceal as much of the underside of paper as possible.

(1)

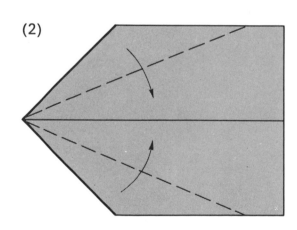

(4)

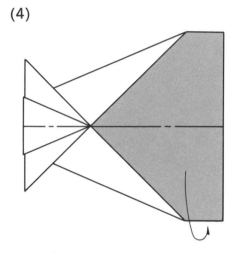

(2)

(5)

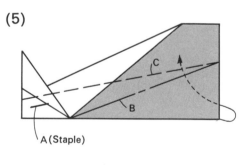

A (Staple)

(3)

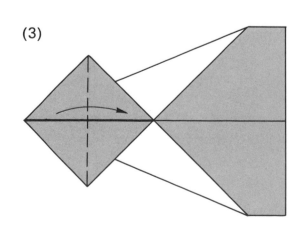

FRONT VIEW

PLAN

Scale : ⅓
Paper Size : A5

SIDE VIEW

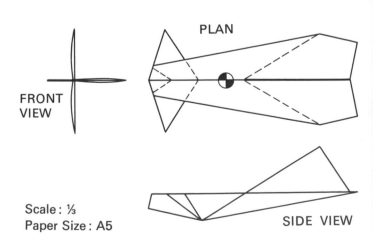

4. FULL-POWER CRAFT

This easy-to-fold airplane is amusing because it can be flown at full strength for high speeds.

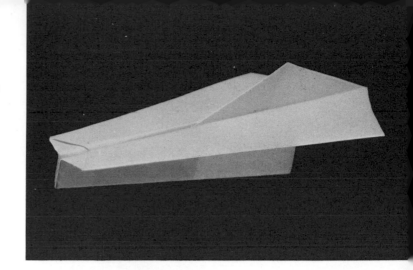

(1)

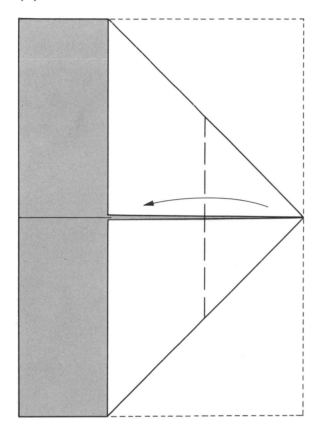

(2)

(3)

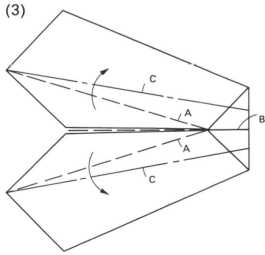

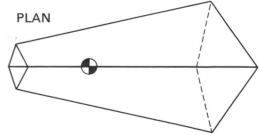

Staple

SIDE VIEW

FRONT VIEW

PLAN

3. First valley fold on lines A then valley fold the model in half on line B. Lower the wings into position by peak folding on lines C. It is a good idea to glue the two sections of the tail together.

Scale : ½
Paper Size : A5

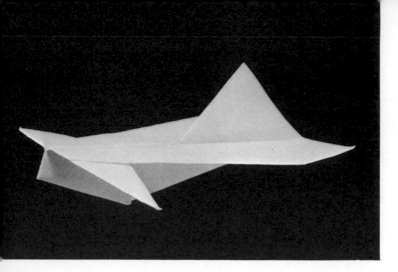

5. NEW SQUID CRAFT

A more creative version, the new squid craft is folded in an entirely different way from older models. For the sake of increased stability, this version uses the entire width of the paper for the forward wings. The shorter fuselage strengthens the structure and moves the center of gravity forward (generally speaking, planes with forward center of gravity fly faster).

(2)

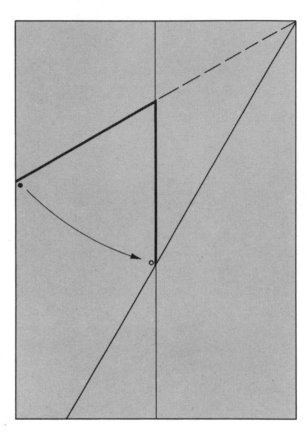

(1)

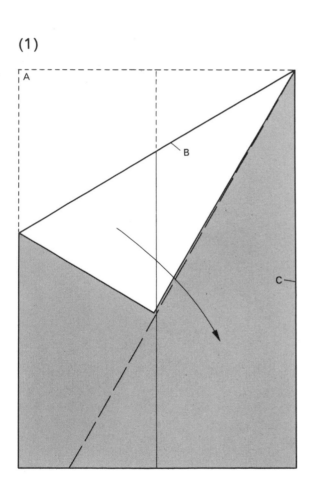

(3)

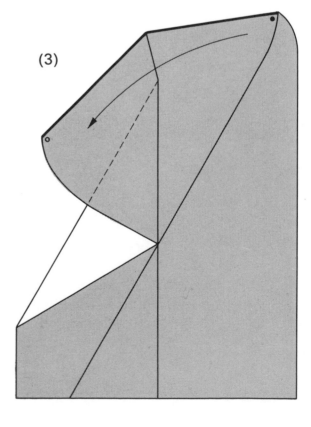

1. Trisecting a right angle.
   Bring point A to the vertical center line. Next fold so that crease B falls on edge C. Then open the paper flat.

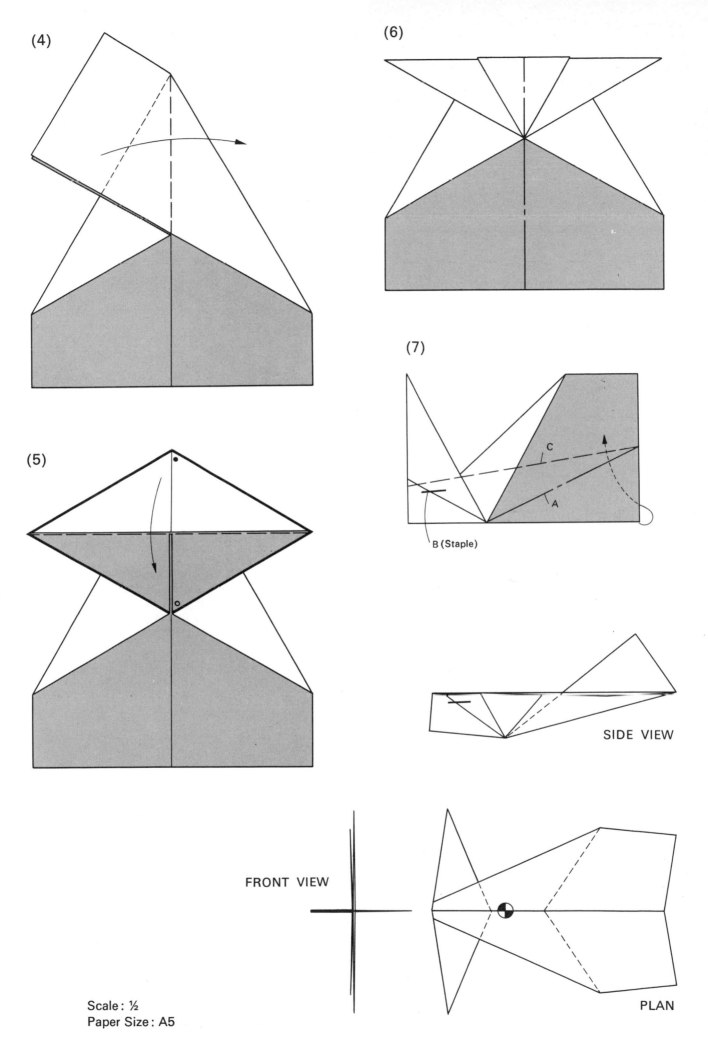

(4)

(5)

(6)

(7)

C

A

B (Staple)

SIDE VIEW

FRONT VIEW

PLAN

Scale: ½
Paper Size: A5

13

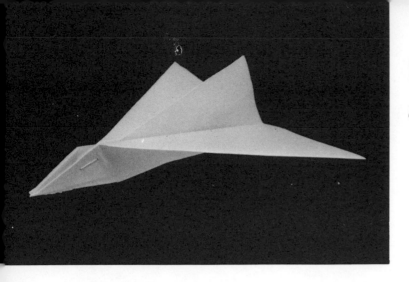

Planes Practical and Possible

6. SINGLE-SEAT FLAT-BODY DELTA CRAFT (TYPE A)

This jet plane has a canopy in the nose section. In making origami airplanes it is important to thicken the leading edges of the wings and the central section. This both strengthens the structure and improves flight dynamics by bringing the paper slightly closer in form to bird feathers or to the wings of real aircraft. This model makes good use of such thickening.

(1)

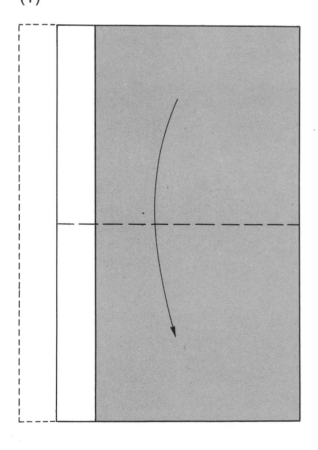

(2)

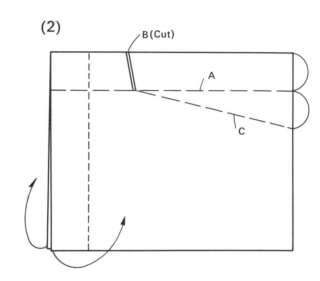

2. Valley fold first on line A; turn the model over and repeat this fold on the other side. Make an incision on line B. Valley fold on line C, which begins at cut B. Turn the model over and repeat.

(3)

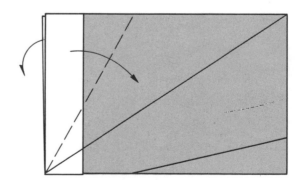

(4)

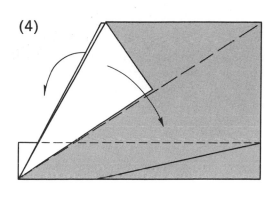

(5)

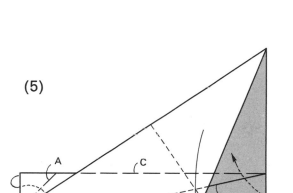

A   C   B

(6)

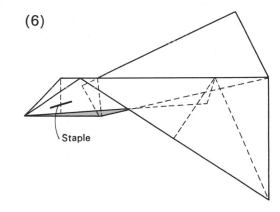

Staple

SIDE VIEW

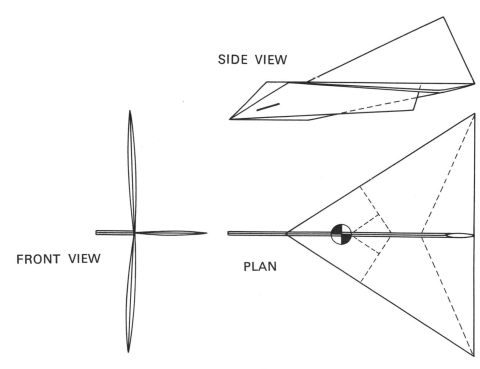

FRONT VIEW

PLAN

Scale: ½
Paper Size: A5

7. SINGLE-SEAT FLAT-BODY DELTA CRAFT (TYPE B—TWO-ENGINE JET)

The two engine nacelles project from the sides of this small delta-wing jet. The general effect of swept-back or delta wings resembles that of wings set at a rising angle. To prevent a duplication of this effect, delta or swept-back wings are usually set at a descending angle.

Folding:

1–2. These steps are identical to steps 1 and 2 in the A type of this plane (p. 14).

(3)

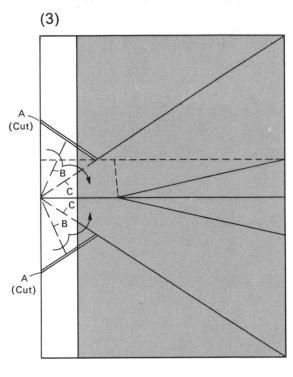

(4)

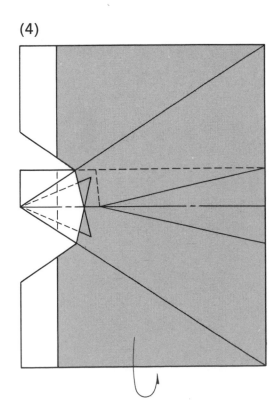

(5)

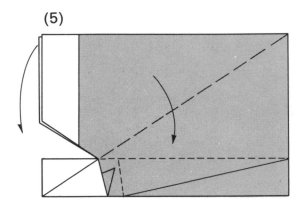

(6)

(7)

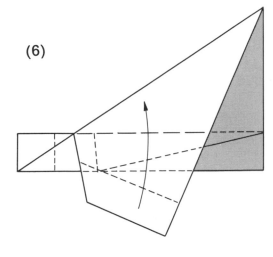

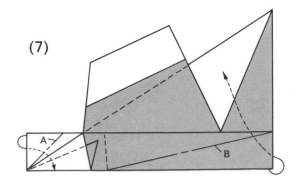

(8)

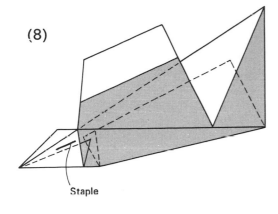

Staple

(9)

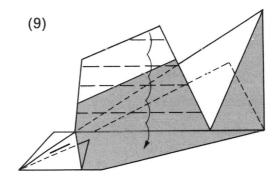

(10)

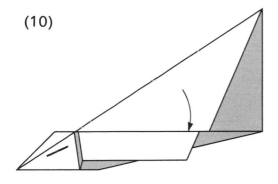

9. Make the small folds necessary to create the engine nacelles. For greater realism, these may be made cylindrical. To achieve this effect wrap them around a square-section stick of suitable size.

Note: Always use plastic-base glue for origami aircraft because it does not become hard when dry and is not subject to great contraction or expansion.

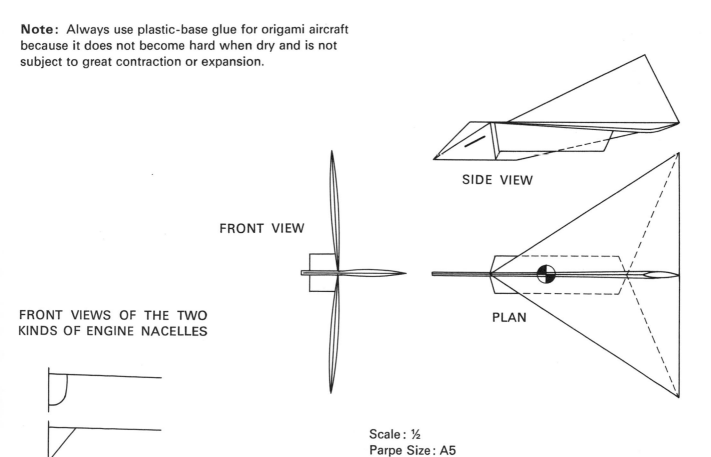

SIDE VIEW

FRONT VIEW

FRONT VIEWS OF THE TWO KINDS OF ENGINE NACELLES

PLAN

Scale: ½
Parpe Size: A5

8. SAAB-37 VIGGEN

This is a version of the world famous plane that is the pride of Sweden. It solves the problem of instability and operational inferiority that plague delta craft flying at low speeds. Furthermore, since the forward wings are placed higher than the main wings, lifting power is improved and turbulent winds on the upper surfaces of the main wings are effectively deflected.

In making the model, keep in mind the characteristics of the real craft. The center of gravity is slightly closer to the front than in most delta craft because of the forward wings.

(1)

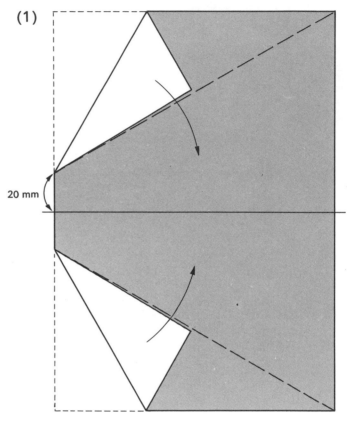

20 mm

(2)

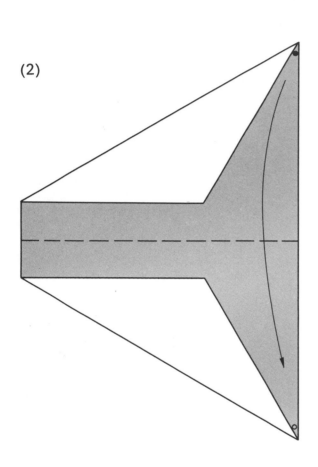

(3)

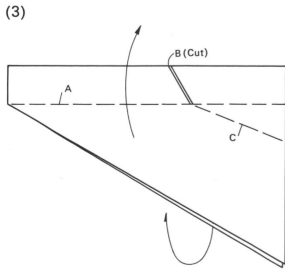

A

B (Cut)

C

(4)

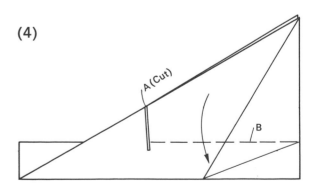

A (Cut)

B

(5)

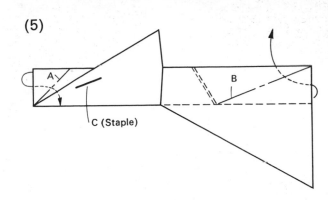

(6)

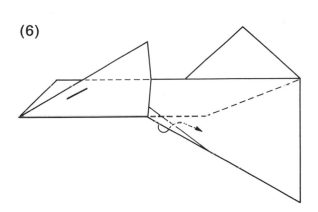

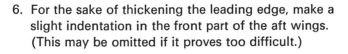

6. For the sake of thickening the leading edge, make a slight indentation in the front part of the aft wings. (This may be omitted if it proves too difficult.)

(8)

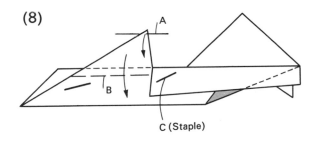

(7)

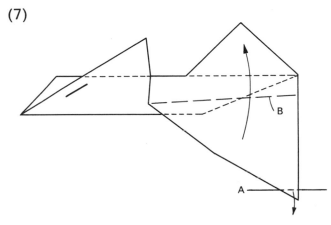

7. Line B is not parallel to the upper edge of the fuselage. It descends slightly to the front to produce what is called a negative angle of attack.

Note: To make this origami plane perform as sharply as cutpaper ones, after you have finished folding it, unfold it and, retracing all steps, glue each fold in place. For very clean lines, weight each fold until it dries then go to the next.

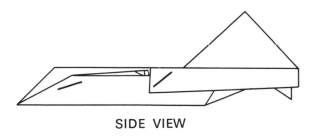

SIDE VIEW

Scale: ½
Paper Size: A5

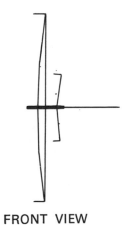

FRONT VIEW

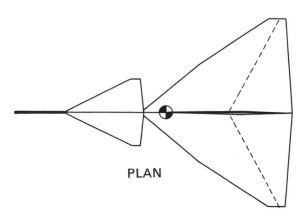

PLAN

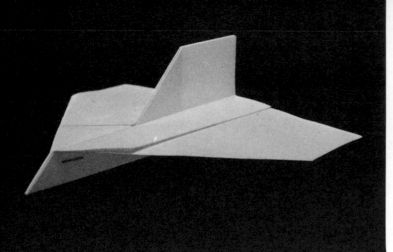

9. GABLE-WING CRAFT (TYPES A AND B)

This model is especially interesting because it is easy and conducive to a number of modifications and improvements. The folding method is a fundamental one that can be used to make many things in addition to airplanes.

TYPE A

(1)

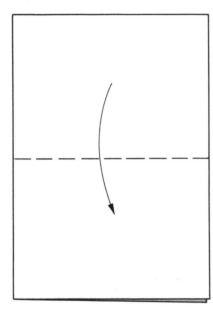

(2)

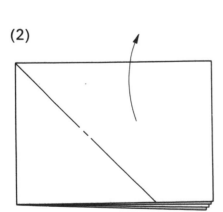

(3)

(4)

(5)

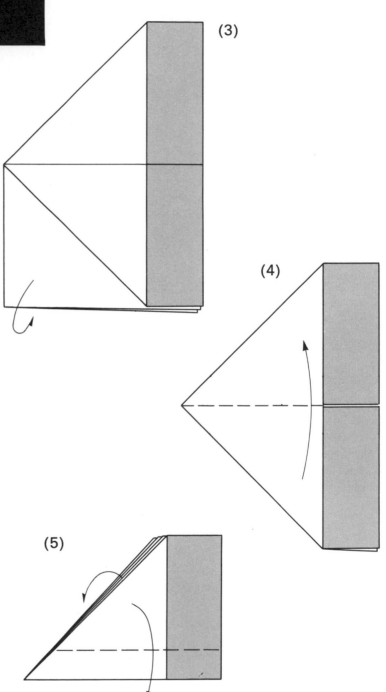

5. Fold the two top layers downward on the broken line. (From this point the instructions divide into one set for the A model and one set for the B model.)

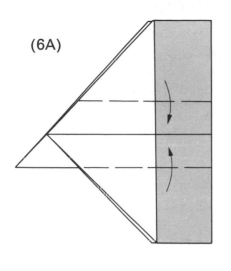

(6A)

TYPE B

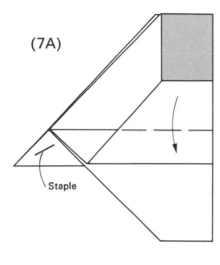

(7A)

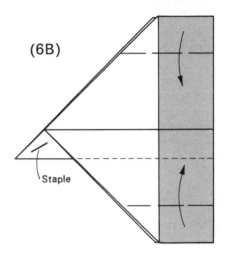

(6B)

6B. After folding as shown, glue the upper and lower layers of each wing together.

7A. After folding as shown, glue the parts of the vertical stabilizer together.

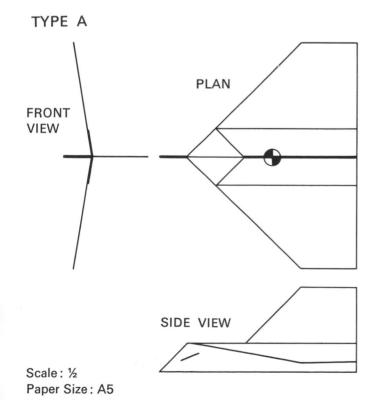

TYPE A

FRONT VIEW

PLAN

SIDE VIEW

Scale : ½
Paper Size : A5

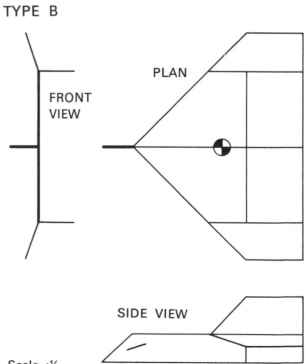

TYPE B

FRONT VIEW

PLAN

SIDE VIEW

Scale : ½
Paper Size : A5

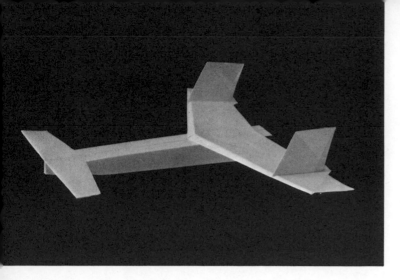

10. STANDARD FORWARD-WING CRAFT

The Canard, or forward-wing craft, has a great many practical good points, but is not yet widely used in aviation. Among the few examples of actual planes of the type are the prewar French Payen and the Swedish

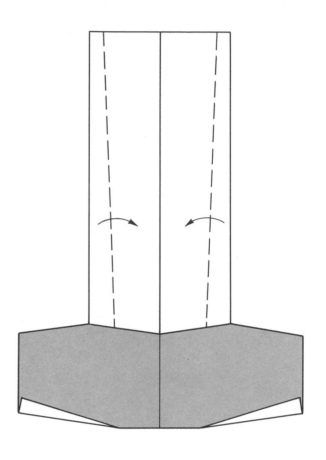

Saab Viggen (p. 18). In origami, however, the forward-wing plane is very popular. The squid plane at the early part of this book (p. 10) is an outstanding version.

Use of this kind of plane would probably greatly reduce air accidents, about 80 per cent of which are connected with landing and takeoff. Furthermore, about 70 per cent of all accidents occurring at these times take place as a result of malfunctions or mistakes during landing. Since this plane has forward wings in addition to main ones to provide lift it need never drag its tail in landing. Because of their numerous advantages the tailless, V-tail, and Canard types will probably become important fields of study in the future.

FORWARD WINGS AND FUSELAGE

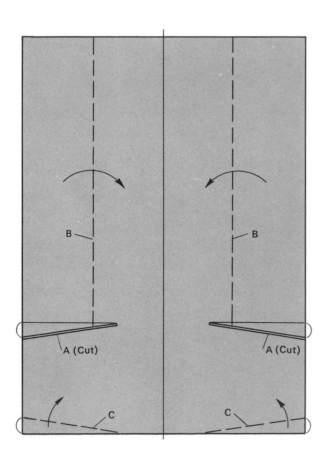

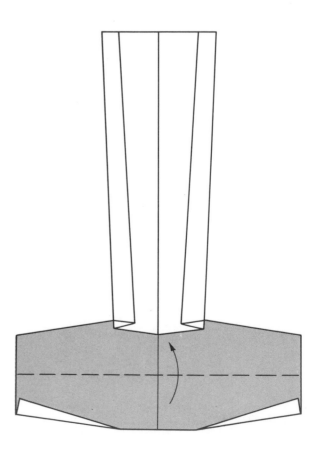

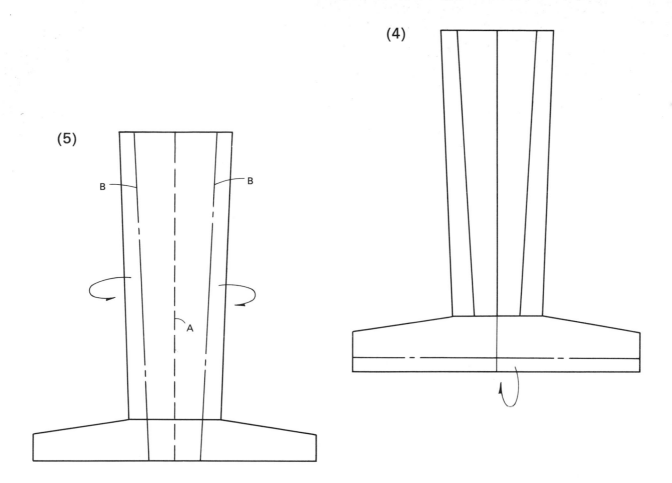

7. Seen from above, the fuselage is the same width throughout its length, but seen from the side it tapers toward the front.

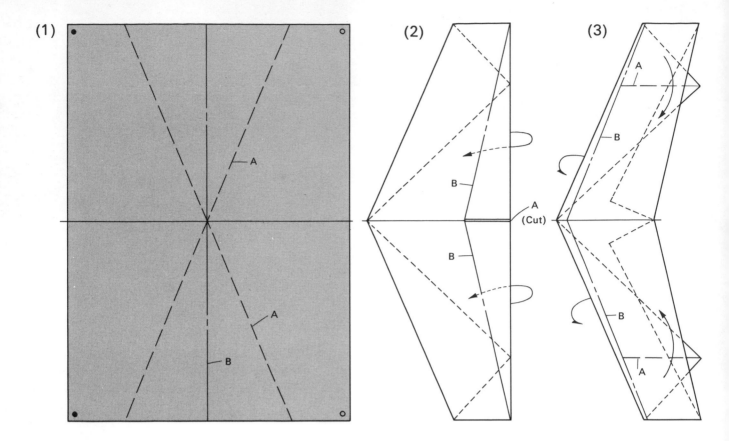

MAIN WINGS

1. Make two intersecting diagonal valley creases A. Fold the paper in half on the long center line. Next pressing inward on the center fold, push the triangular sections formed by the diagonals inward.

3. Valley fold on lines A of the top layers only to produce vertical stabilizers on the wing tips. Roll the leading edge under slightly for added lift power.

Assembly: Add small amounts of glue on the leading and trailing edges of the main wings at points that will correspond to the edges of the fuselage. Attach the two.

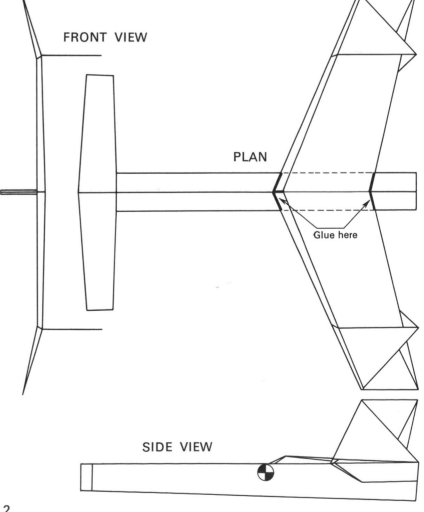

Scale: ½
Paper Size: A5 × 2

11. CLASSIC BIPLANE

In the early days of the airplane, craft with several wings were considered most rational from the standpoints of materials strength and technical planning; some of them had three or more sets of wings. Today, however, the monoplane reigns supreme, and the biplane has all but vanished. Since attempting to make biplanes with a single sheet of paper involves so much cutting that the origami value of the model dwindles to virtually nothing, I have used a compound folding method. It took many years of study to develop a folding method for producing both sets of wings from one sheet of paper. In this case, the lower wings are considerably shorter than the upper ones. To make them the same length seriously impairs the aircraft's performance. Because the two parts of the model may be moved forward or backward at will, adjustment of the center of gravity is a simple matter.

(1)

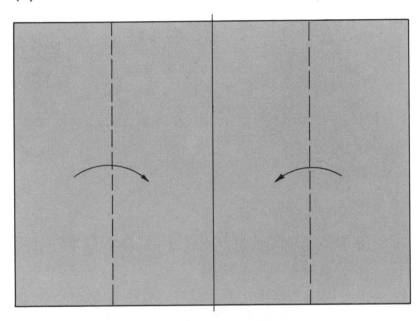

FUSELAGE

(2)

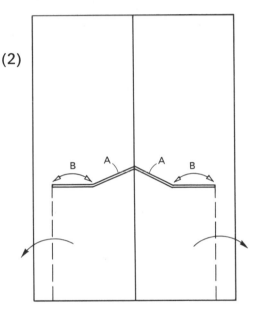

2. Make the V-shaped cut labeled A in both the upper and lower layers of the paper. Make the cuts labeled B in the upper layer only.

(3)

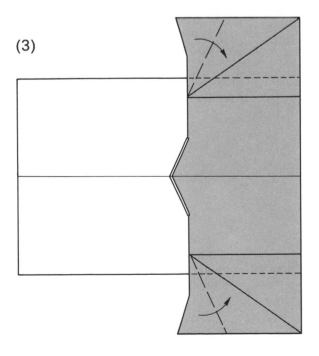

(4)

(5)

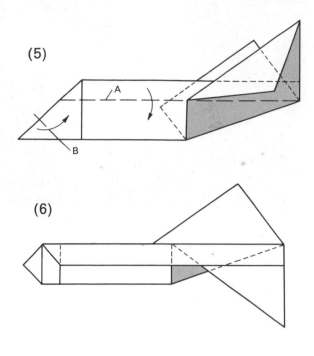

(6)

(7)

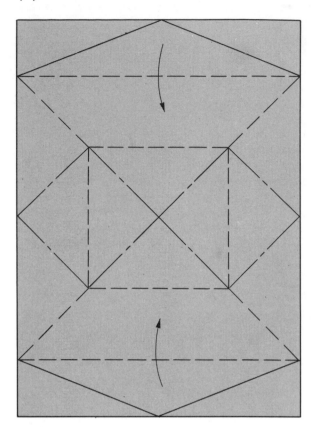

MAIN WINGS

1–4. Fold the gable-shaped craft (p. 20) to step 4.

7. Make all the creases shown.

(5)

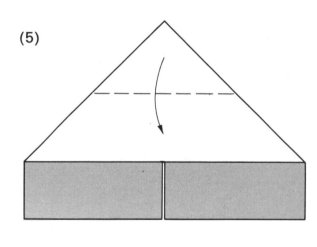

(6)

(8)

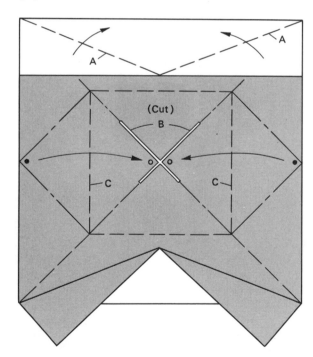

5–6. Valley fold the top triangle; make sharp creases. Then open the entire figure.

8. Bring the black dots to the white dots; this will automatically pull all four sides of the figure to the center.

(9)

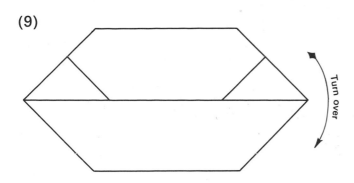

Turn over

(10)

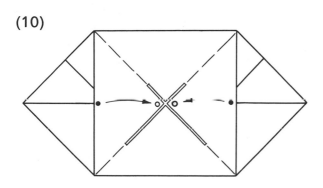

(11)

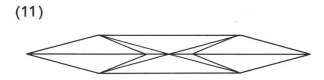

(12)

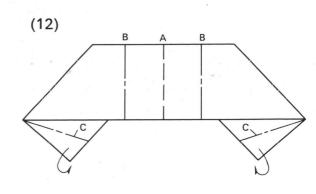

(13)

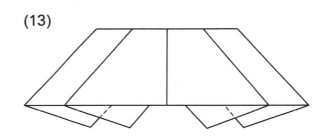

10–11. Once again pull the sides toward the center X. The figure looks like this from the top; turn it on its side.

Assembly: Insert the fuselage in the X-shaped opening between the wings.

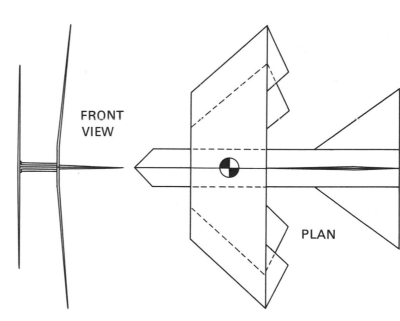

FRONT VIEW

PLAN

Note: In combining the wings and the fuselage, do not apply glue at the points of junction between them (places with X-shaped slits).

Scale: ½
Paper Size: A5 × 2

SIDE VIEW

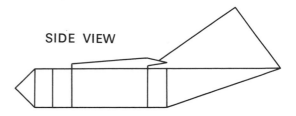

27

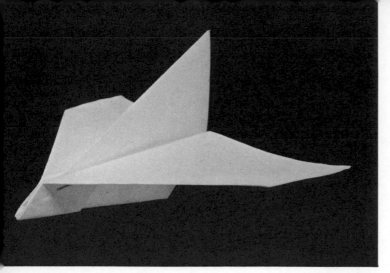

12. ARROW-FEATHER DELTA CRAFT

The characteristics of this plane are the wingspread, which employs the full diagonal of a true-rectangle, and the tail with its backswept trailing edge. This flying origami substantiates my claim that the true-rectangle is an excellent geometric figure for origami purposes, for the apparent excess formed when the sheet of paper is folded on the diagonal actually strengthens the plane and improves the cross section of the wings. This goes to show that the true-rectangle is proof that there is no waste in the world of nature. Since the folding method is a fundamental one used in making origami birds and insects, it deserves special attention and practice.

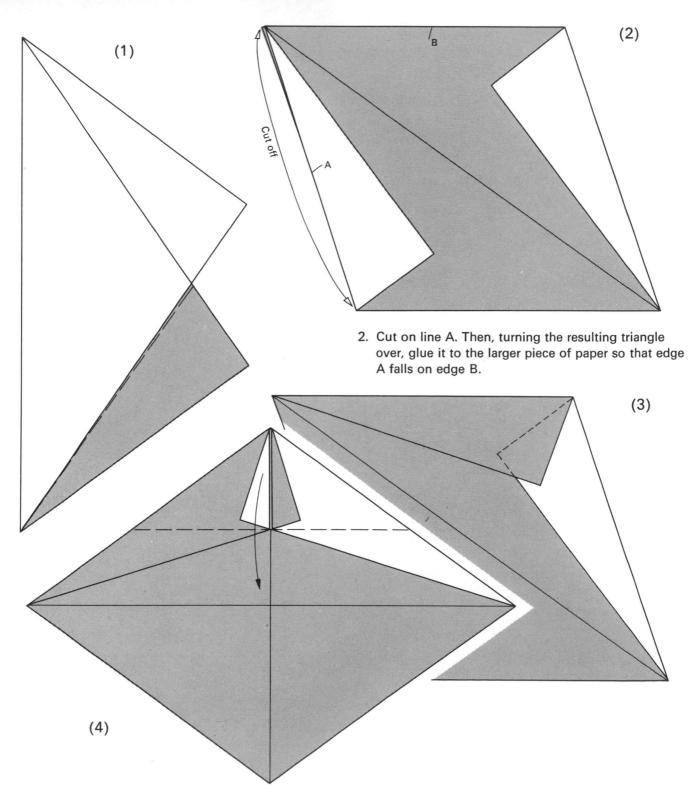

2. Cut on line A. Then, turning the resulting triangle over, glue it to the larger piece of paper so that edge A falls on edge B.

(1)

(2)

(3)

(4)

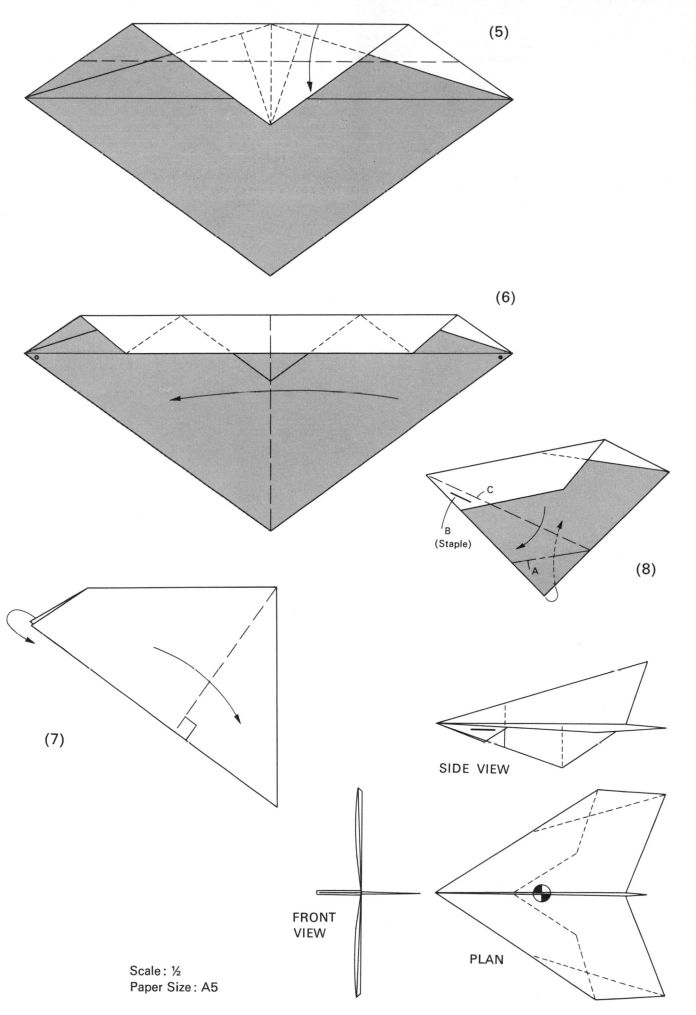

(5)

(6)

(7)

(8)

C

B
(Staple)

A

SIDE VIEW

FRONT
VIEW

PLAN

Scale: ½
Paper Size: A5

13. V-TAIL CRAFT

There are no large V-tail craft, though the type appears often in small planes and soarers—a kind of glider. Because its structure is simple and because it has no true vertical stabilizer, the V-tail reduces air resistance. It is difficult to make a vertical stabilizer in one piece with the fuselage in origami aircraft. For that reason, one must either adopt the forward-wing style and use the wings as the vertical stabilizer or use the V-tail design. With a little investigation, it might be possible to develop a simpler version of this plane that differs from the preceding delta craft.

FUSELAGE

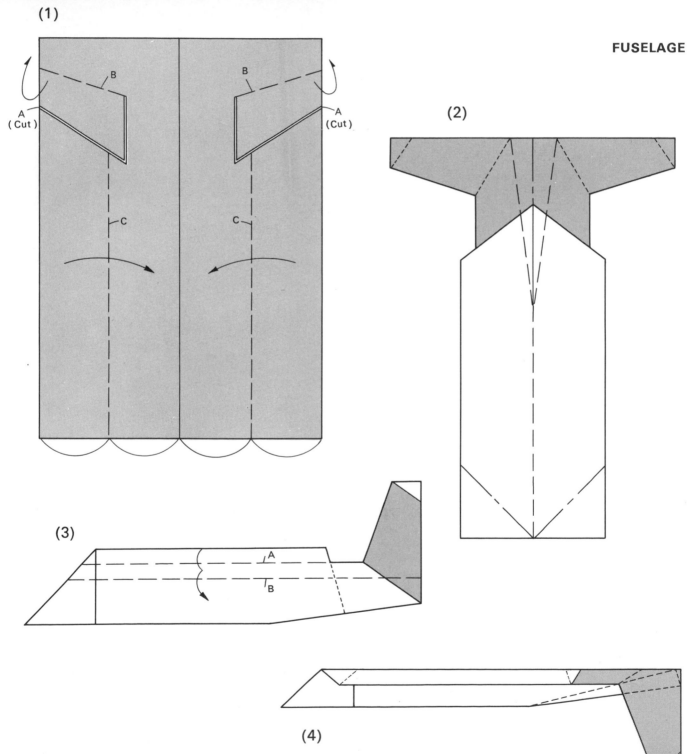

(1)

(2)

(3)

(4)

MAIN WINGS

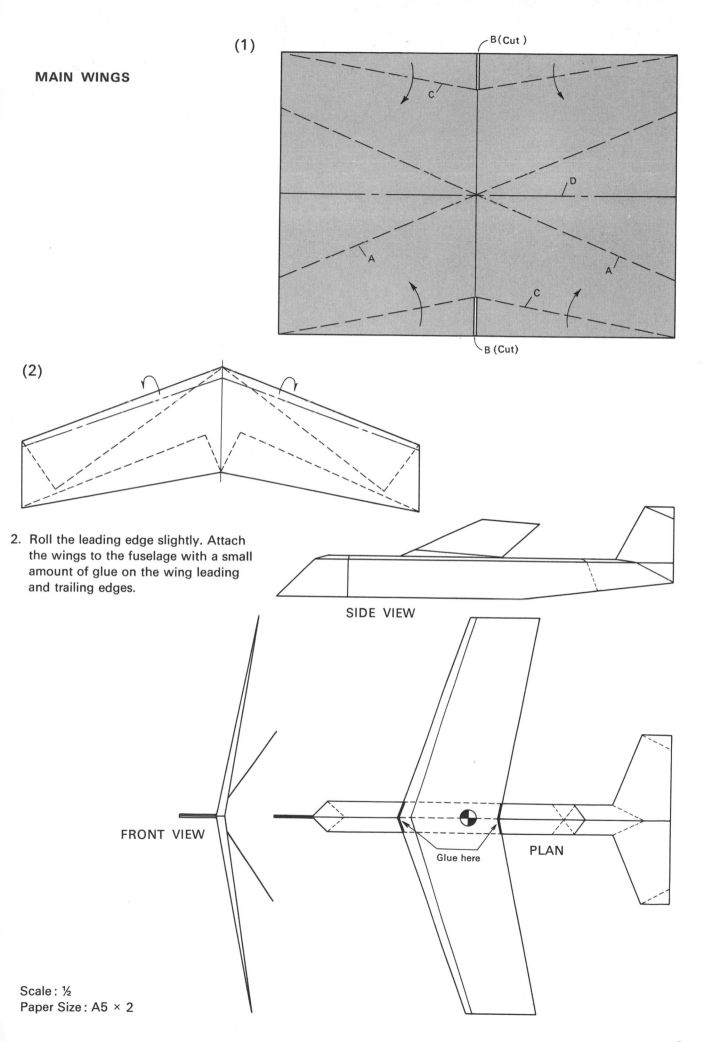

(1)

B(Cut)

C

D

A

A

C

B (Cut)

(2)

2. Roll the leading edge slightly. Attach the wings to the fuselage with a small amount of glue on the wing leading and trailing edges.

SIDE VIEW

FRONT VIEW

Glue here

PLAN

Scale: ½
Paper Size: A5 × 2

Planes
for the Future

14.   LIFTING-BODY DYNA-SOA

At first glance, this origami version of the American masterpiece, the Dyna-soa, looks difficult to fold, but with repeated practice it becomes much easier.

Since the entire fuselage is dynamically designed to provide lift, even when it is returning from the outer atmosphere to earth, it requires no wings to land at a fixed location. It can be attached to the tip of a rocket, or slung below the fuselage of a large aircraft. Although the origami version is composed largely of

Paper after Creasing

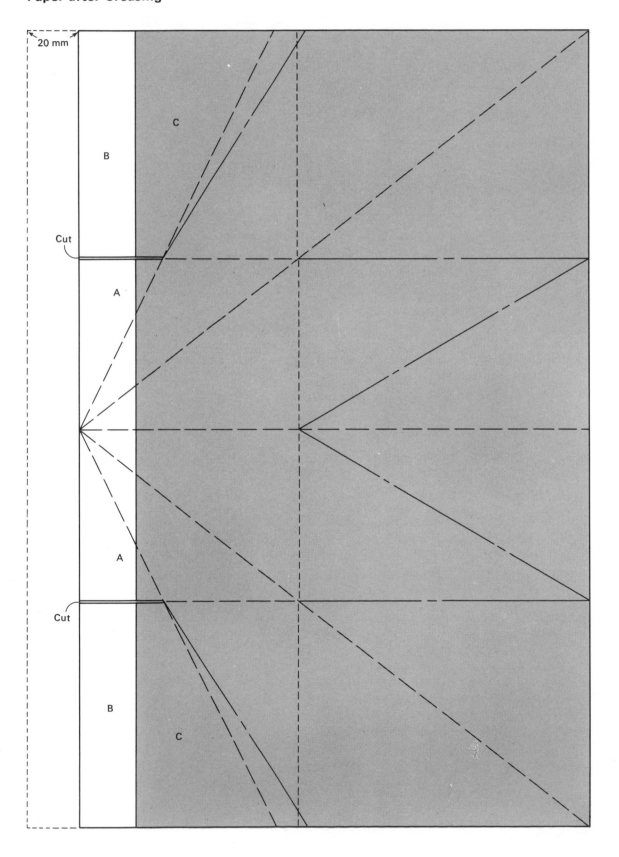

straight lines, it preserves the general appearance of the original. If folded properly, the origami Dyna-soa performs excellently. It is especially interesting because it has no wings.

In this case I have shown all of the folds that appear in the paper when a completed origami Dyna-soa is unfolded. Since the number of folds is small, approach the plane as if it were your own creation.

Pre-folding: First valley fold on a line 2 cm from the left edge and glue flap in place. Next, cut a piece of paper of the same thickness and wide enough to reach from the fold in the left edge to the dotted line. Glue this strip to the larger piece of paper.

Actual Size
Paper Size: A5

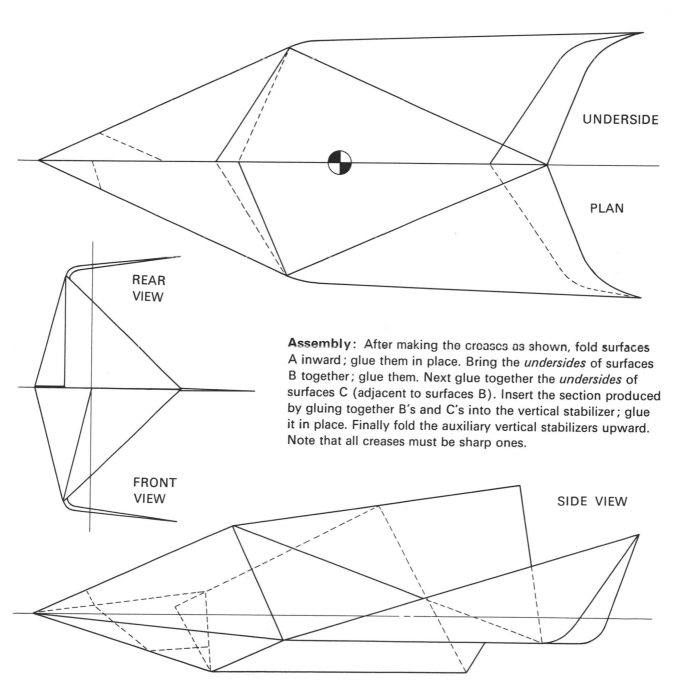

UNDERSIDE

PLAN

REAR VIEW

FRONT VIEW

SIDE VIEW

Assembly: After making the creases as shown, fold surfaces A inward; glue them in place. Bring the *undersides* of surfaces B together; glue them. Next glue together the *undersides* of surfaces C (adjacent to surfaces B). Insert the section produced by gluing together B's and C's into the vertical stabilizer; glue it in place. Finally fold the auxiliary vertical stabilizers upward. Note that all creases must be sharp ones.

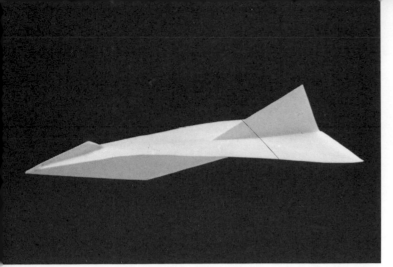

15. SPACE SHUTTLE (TYPES A AND B)

In the future, shuttle craft like these two will be used together with other space ships for travel and transport in and out of the earth's atmosphere. Designed largely for use in outer space, the shuttle will not launch immediately from the earth. Instead it will be combined with tailless craft, which will serve as wings for the shuttle. When the two have reached a certain altitude, the wings will be detached and the shuttle will fly to outer space. The tailless craft can either wait to dock with the returning shuttle, or it can return alone to the earth. Although the real space shuttle does not require a tail as large as this one, the origami version needs it for satisfactory performance.

TYPE B

Paper after Creasing

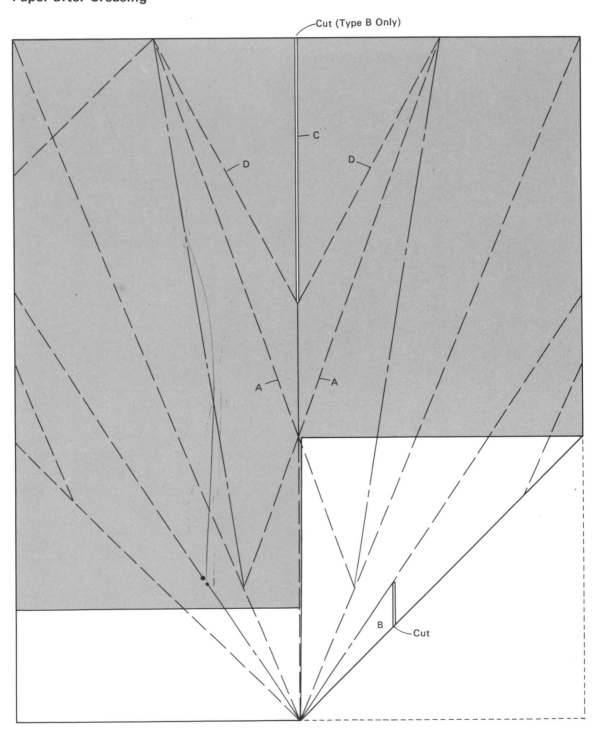

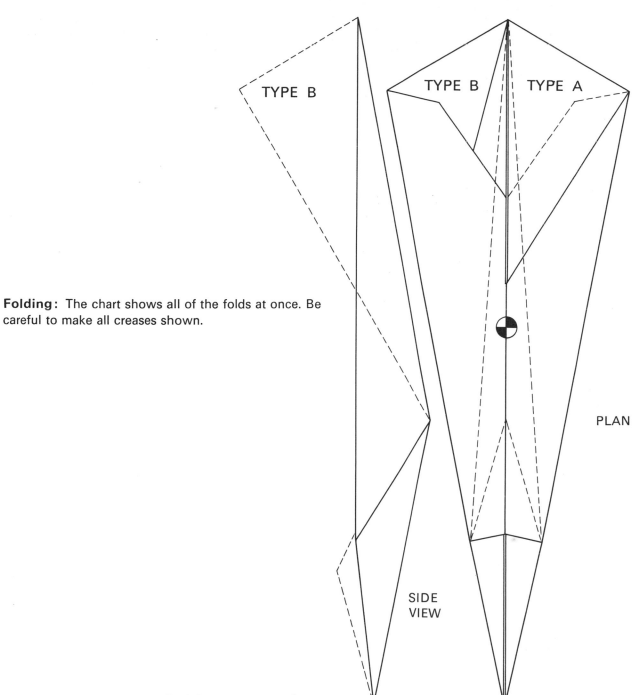

Folding: The chart shows all of the folds at once. Be careful to make all creases shown.

TYPE B

TYPE B TYPE A

PLAN

SIDE
VIEW

Assembly: After making all of these creases and incisions, assemble the plane according to them so that it is symmetrical. The triangle formed by lines A becomes the tail section, and the smaller triangle B becomes the elevating canopy.

Space shuttle type B is made like type A except that a vertical stabilizer is needed. To achieve this effect, make a slit on line C as shown and fold outward on lines D.

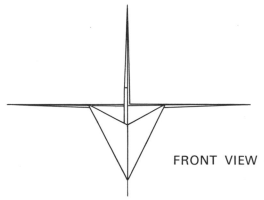

FRONT VIEW

Actual Size
Paper Size: A5

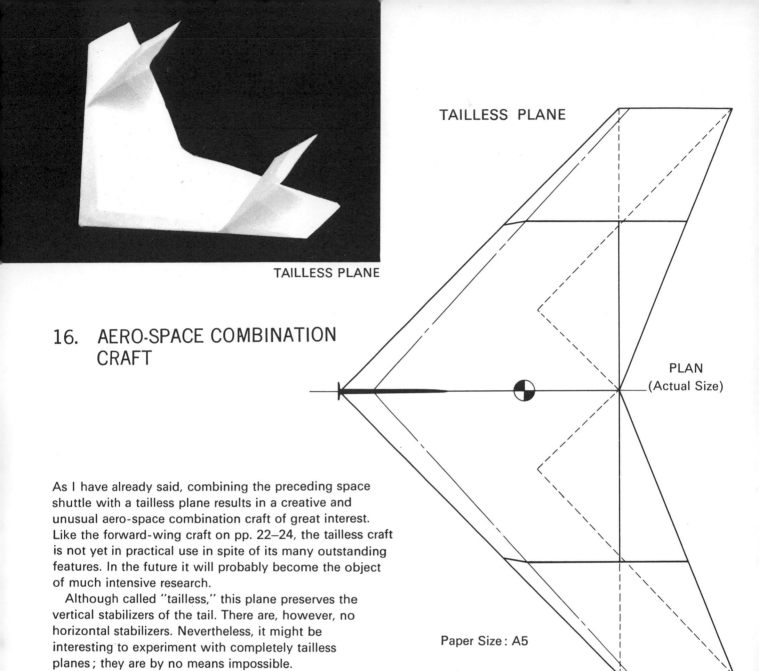

TAILLESS PLANE

PLAN
(Actual Size)

Paper Size: A5

TAILLESS PLANE

16. AERO-SPACE COMBINATION CRAFT

As I have already said, combining the preceding space shuttle with a tailless plane results in a creative and unusual aero-space combination craft of great interest. Like the forward-wing craft on pp. 22–24, the tailless craft is not yet in practical use in spite of its many outstanding features. In the future it will probably become the object of much intensive research.

Although called "tailless," this plane preserves the vertical stabilizers of the tail. There are, however, no horizontal stabilizers. Nevertheless, it might be interesting to experiment with completely tailless planes; they are by no means impossible.

Folding: Fold the gable-shape plane (p. 20) to step 4. Make a slit on the long center line. The corners of the flaps formed by these cuts must be inserted within the body of the plane. Glue them in place. Make the vertical stabilizers by valley folding the top layer of the paper only. Roll the entire leading edge of the craft slightly downward.

Note: Rolling the leading edge strengthens the craft and adds lift power. Twist the trailing edge upward slightly so that it serves as an upper rudder. Weight the plane by inserting a nail about 1 in. in the nose and gluing it in position. To fly the plane, rest it on the thumb and middle finger and, pressing the top of the trailing edge lightly with the index finger, launch it.

The aero-space combination is formed of this tailless plane and the preceding space shuttle type A. The tailless plane becomes the main wings of the combination. In such a case, bend the tips of the wings of the tailless craft slightly upward. The two may be joined by glue placed on the leading and trailing edges of the tailless craft wings. The glue must be spaced no farther apart than the width of the fuselage of the space shuttle.

AERO-SPACE COMBINATION CRAFT

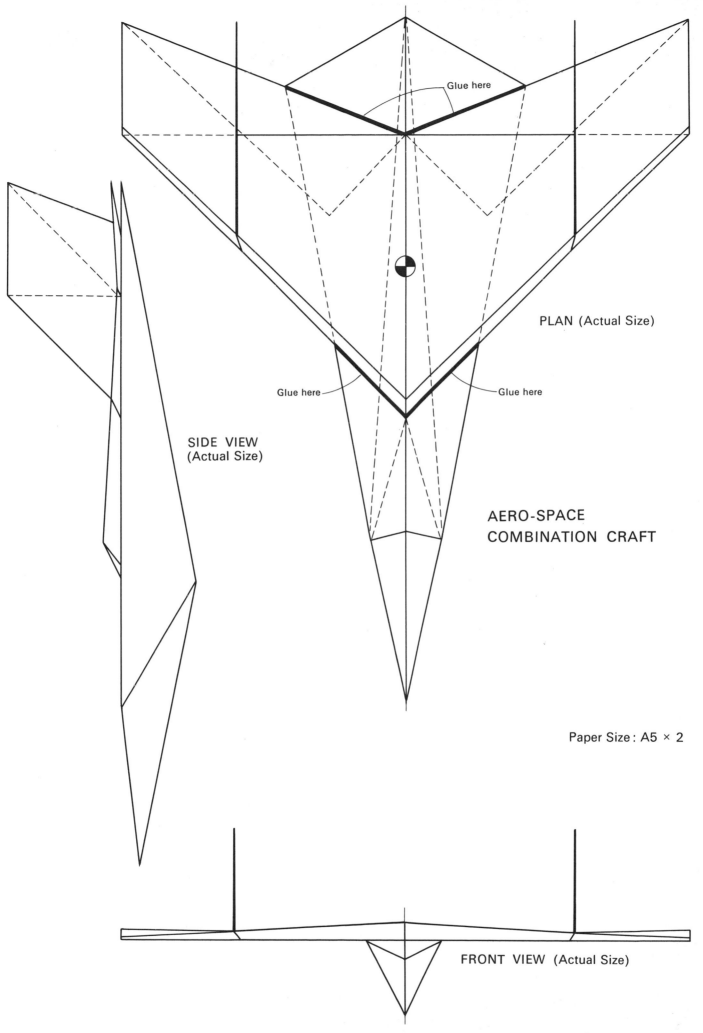

Glue here

PLAN (Actual Size)

Glue here   Glue here

SIDE VIEW
(Actual Size)

AERO-SPACE
COMBINATION CRAFT

Paper Size : A5 × 2

FRONT VIEW (Actual Size)

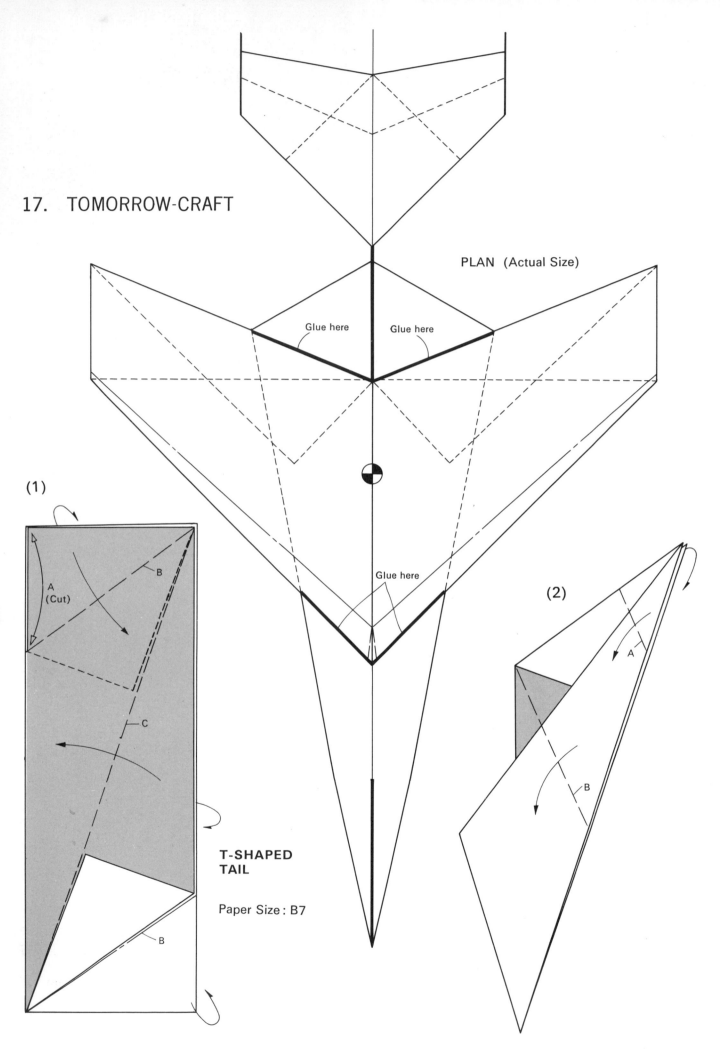

17. TOMORROW-CRAFT

PLAN (Actual Size)

Glue here   Glue here

Glue here

(1)

A
(Cut)

B

C

B

**T-SHAPED
TAIL**

Paper Size : B7

(2)

A

B

38

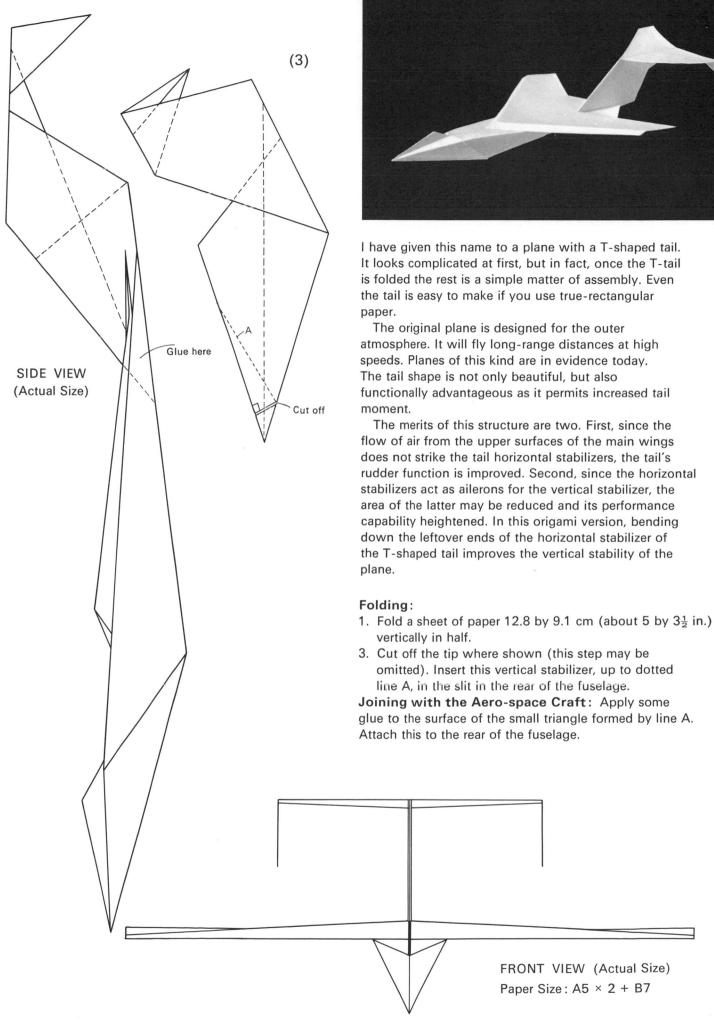

(3)

SIDE VIEW
(Actual Size)

Glue here

A

Cut off

I have given this name to a plane with a T-shaped tail. It looks complicated at first, but in fact, once the T-tail is folded the rest is a simple matter of assembly. Even the tail is easy to make if you use true-rectangular paper.

The original plane is designed for the outer atmosphere. It will fly long-range distances at high speeds. Planes of this kind are in evidence today. The tail shape is not only beautiful, but also functionally advantageous as it permits increased tail moment.

The merits of this structure are two. First, since the flow of air from the upper surfaces of the main wings does not strike the tail horizontal stabilizers, the tail's rudder function is improved. Second, since the horizontal stabilizers act as ailerons for the vertical stabilizer, the area of the latter may be reduced and its performance capability heightened. In this origami version, bending down the leftover ends of the horizontal stabilizer of the T-shaped tail improves the vertical stability of the plane.

Folding:
1. Fold a sheet of paper 12.8 by 9.1 cm (about 5 by 3½ in.) vertically in half.
3. Cut off the tip where shown (this step may be omitted). Insert this vertical stabilizer, up to dotted line A, in the slit in the rear of the fuselage.

Joining with the Aero-space Craft: Apply some glue to the surface of the small triangle formed by line A. Attach this to the rear of the fuselage.

FRONT VIEW (Actual Size)
Paper Size: A5 × 2 + B7

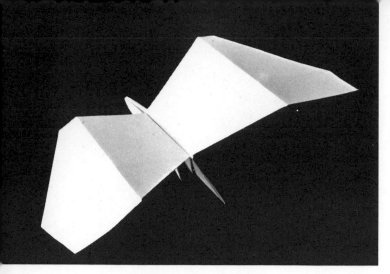

18. FLUTTERING BIRD

Turning for a while from airplanes, I should like to introduce a few flying creature. The first is this fluttering bird. The ideal paper for this origami is art paper—the kind that is glossy on both sides—and the ideal flying conditions are indoors on a rainy day. This is because when the paper has absorbed a great deal of moisture the bird's wings make a pleasant flapping sound. By giving the outer part of the wings slightly more downward twist (washout) than is ordinarily needed, it is possible to set up what is called flutter in aircraft. This makes the origami look more real in flight. Because the flapping is not natural, however, but is the result of treatment of the shape and angle of the wings, you must not expect this bird to fly very far. It would be a good idea for you to study the reasons for the fluttering phenomenon and perhaps devise a better version of this origami.

(1)

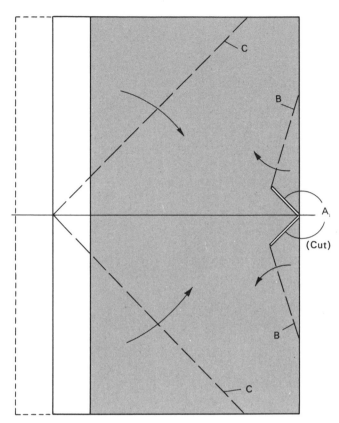

(2)

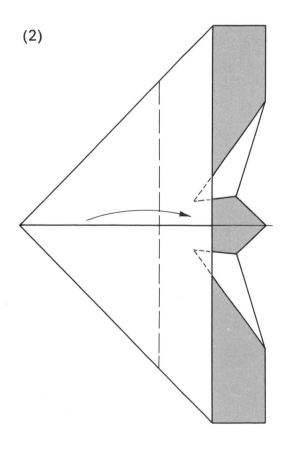

(3)

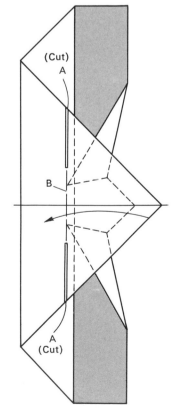

(4)

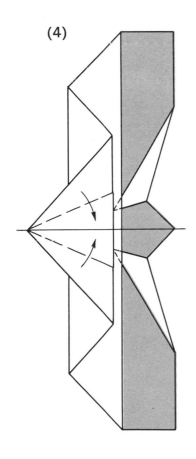

(5)

Turn over

(6)

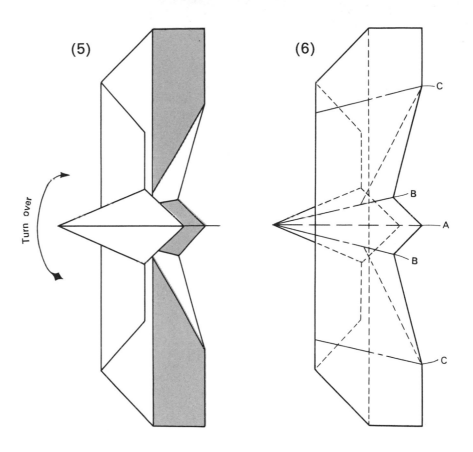

6. First fold the entire body in half on center line A. Next separate the wings from the body by peak folding on lines B. Make the outer wings by peak folding on lines C; these folds must parallel those on lines B.

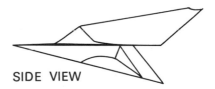

SIDE VIEW

Note: Twist the wings so that their upper surfaces seem to be larger at the outer edge. Test fly the bird. If it performs well, further twist the wings upward to produce the fluttering effect.

FRONT VIEW

PLAN

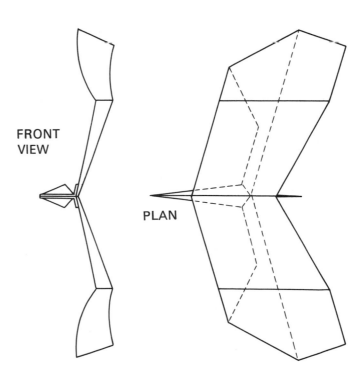

Scale: ½
Paper Size: A5

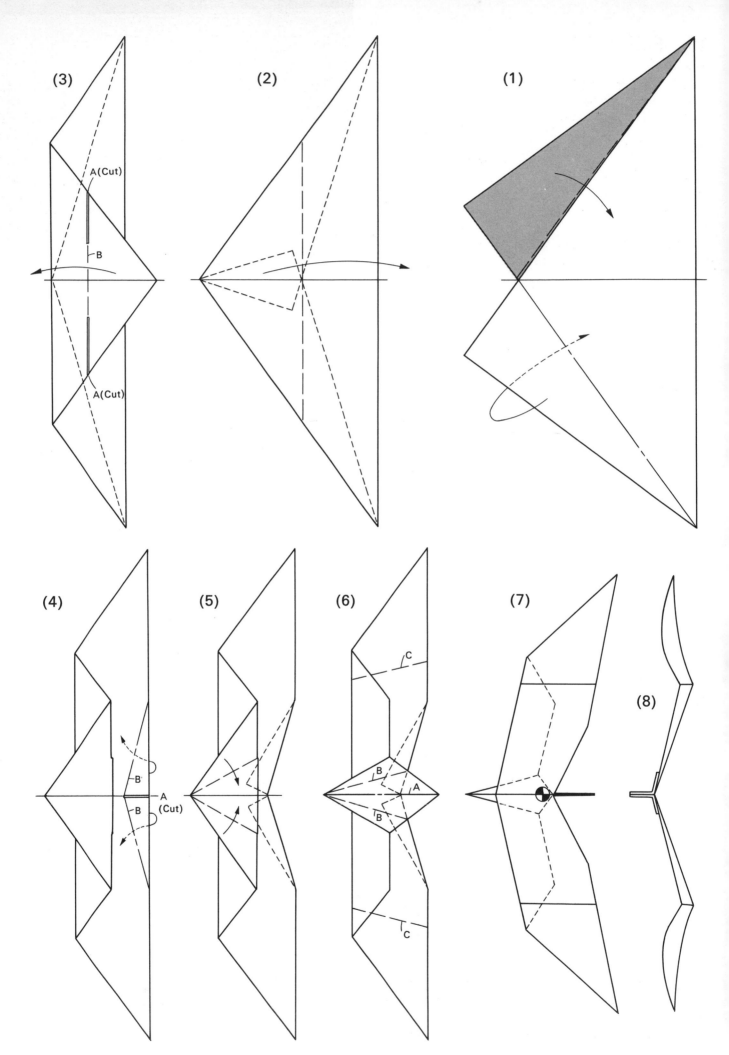

19. FLUTTERING SEAGULL

Although the principle on which it flies is similar to that used in the preceding fluttering bird, this seagull is more realistic because it flaps its wings more slowly. Many medium birds, like the seagull, have wingspans that are large for their bodies. Consequently in ordinary flight they soar or glide and reserve energetic wing movements for takeoffs, landings, and bad-weather flying. Even then, however, the wing movement is less the fluttering of smaller birds than a slow, graceful sweeping motion.

The length of the wings of this origami seagull permits suitably slow movement, but if the washout in the wing tips is too great, instead of waving its wings, the whole seagull will rise and fall a few times and then suddenly drop to the floor. For the sake of realistic flying, adjust the wings carefully. It is possible to attach a tail section to the seagull.

Folding:

4. Make the slit shown at A. Insert the four resulting flaps inside the wings.

VARIATION

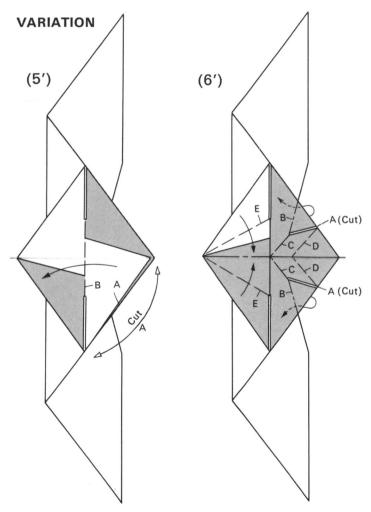

(5')   (6')

FRONT VIEW

PLAN

SIDE VIEW

Scale: ½
Paper Size: A5

VARIATION: These steps make it possible to add a tail section. After making the incision in step 3, fold over the top layer only.

5'. Make the slits shown on line A; valley fold on line B.

20. GLIDING DRAGONFLY

Of course, unlike traditional origami dragonflies, these actually fly. Because the dragonfly is later in evolutionary development than many other insects, its wings permit more variable angle adjustment. For instance, in contrast to the butterflies and cicadas, whose front and back wings move simultaneously and in the same directions, the dragonfly's front wings are tipped slightly up and the somewhat backswept rear ones are tilted down. Furthermore the dragonfly can move its wings in alternation. This enables it to generate lift under most circumstances, to fly in straight lines, and to hang motionless in the air.

Of course, all this is too much to expect of origami, but this paper model glides very nicely. To achieve this, I have tilted the forward wings upward and the rear ones downward and have added stability by twisting the tips of the rear wings down. The center of gravity is placed about two-thirds the width of the combined front and back wings from the leading edge of the front pair. The downward twist in the tips of the rear set of wings improves stability.

Note: This is probably the most difficult origami in this book. Use large thin paper to practice with. Fold slowly and accurately two or three times, and you are certain to succeed.

Folding:

1–2. Fold as in step 1 and 2 of the seagull (p. 42) then open the center fold.

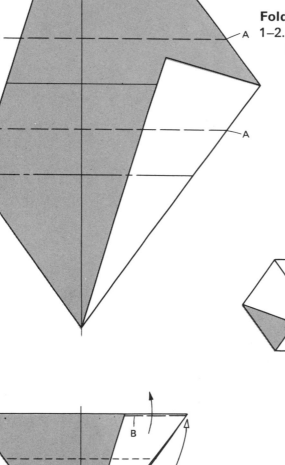

(3)

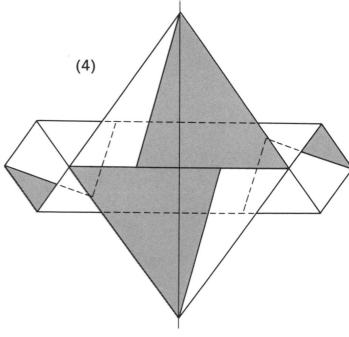

(4)

(5)

5. Cut the folded edge of line A. Apply a thin coat of glue to the area labeled and lifting it upward, glue it to the upper larger triangle section.

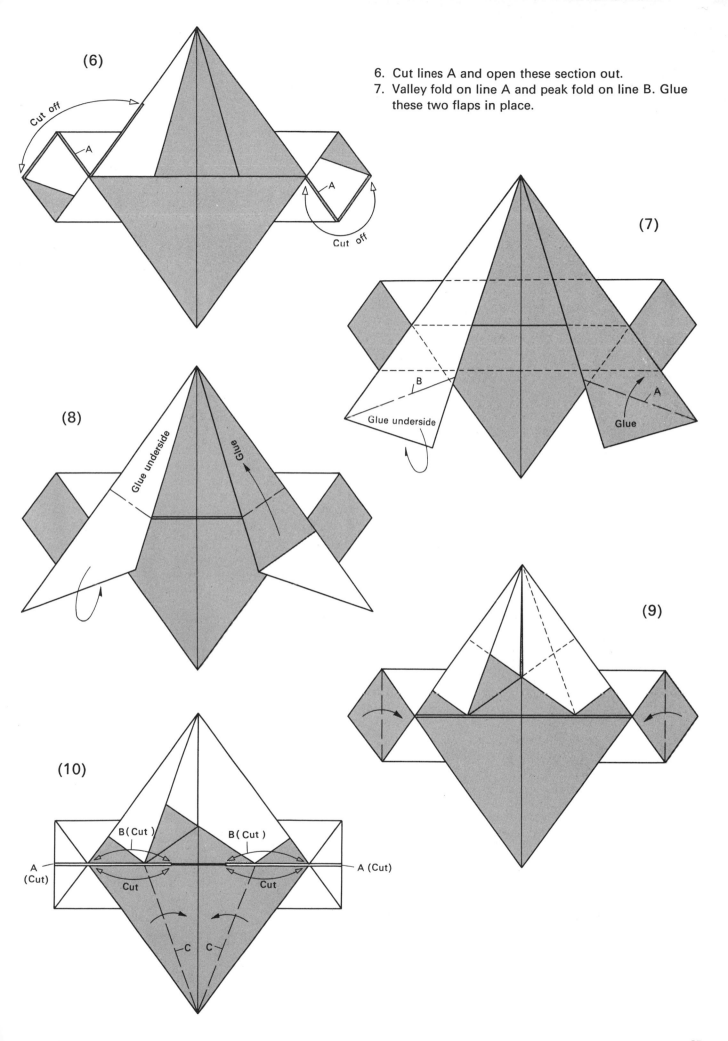

(6)

Cut off

A

Cut off

6. Cut lines A and open these section out.
7. Valley fold on line A and peak fold on line B. Glue these two flaps in place.

(7)

B

Glue underside

Glue

A

(8)

Glue underside

Glue

(9)

(10)

B (Cut)   B (Cut)

A
(Cut)   A (Cut)

Cut   Cut

C   C

45

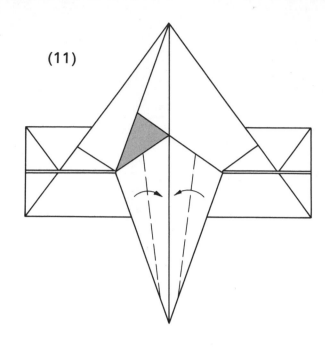

(11)

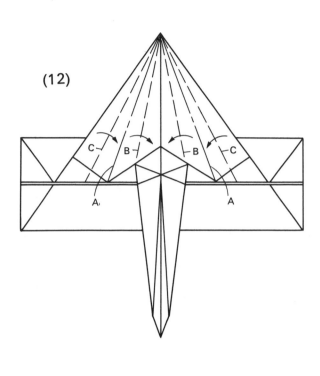

(12)

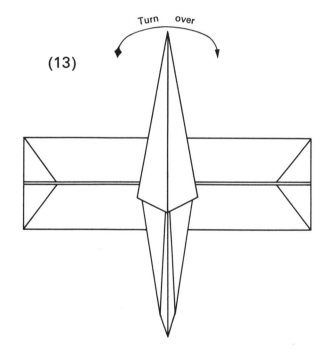

(13)

Turn over

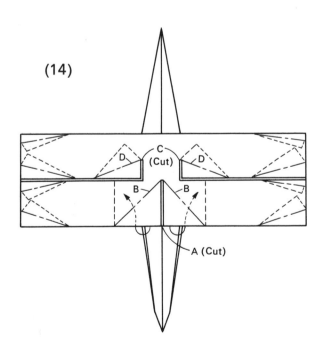

(14)

14. Note that the flaps at the bases of the wings are inserted in the wings.

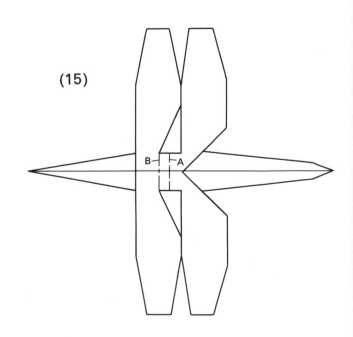

(15)

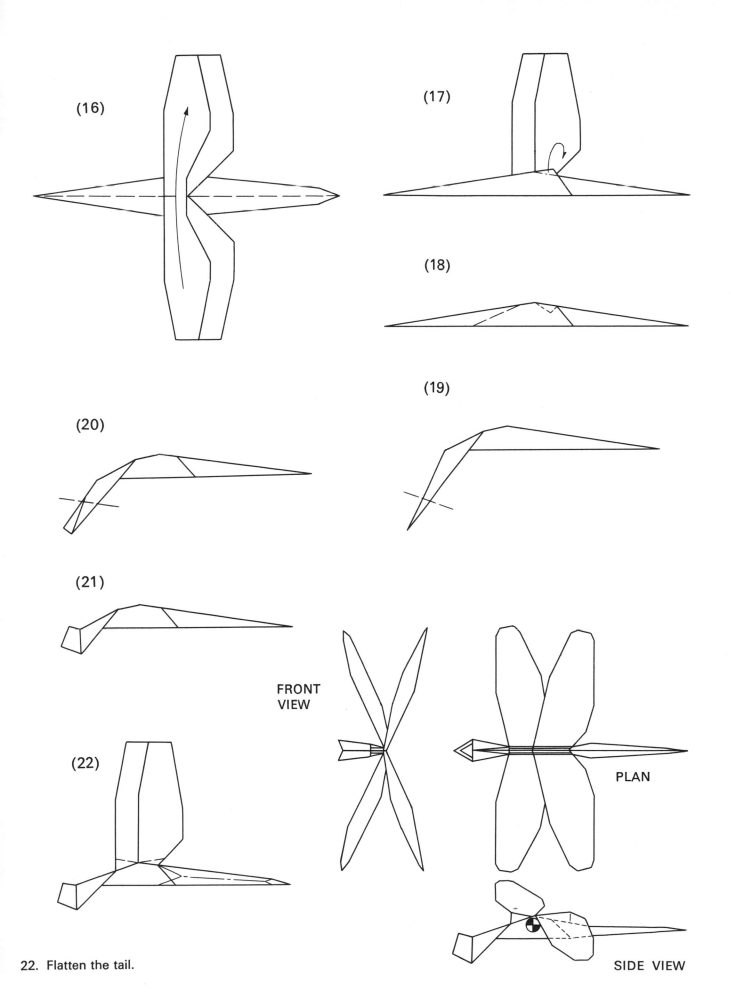

(16)

(17)

(18)

(19)

(20)

(21)

(22)

FRONT VIEW

PLAN

SIDE VIEW

22. Flatten the tail.

Scale: ½
Paper Size: A5

21. DRAGONFLY AT REST

This stationary origami is designed as a companion piece for the flying one. It shows the position dragonflies assume when resting for a brief period. For extended rests they move their wings much farther forward. Since this model is made very much like the preceding one, I have explained only the points of difference between the two. The numbered steps in this fold correspond with those in the preceding dragonfly.

Folding:
Steps 1 through 6, 11 through 17, and 19 through 22 are the same as in the preceding dragonfly.

7. Pull out the parts in which the necessary slits have been made in step 6.

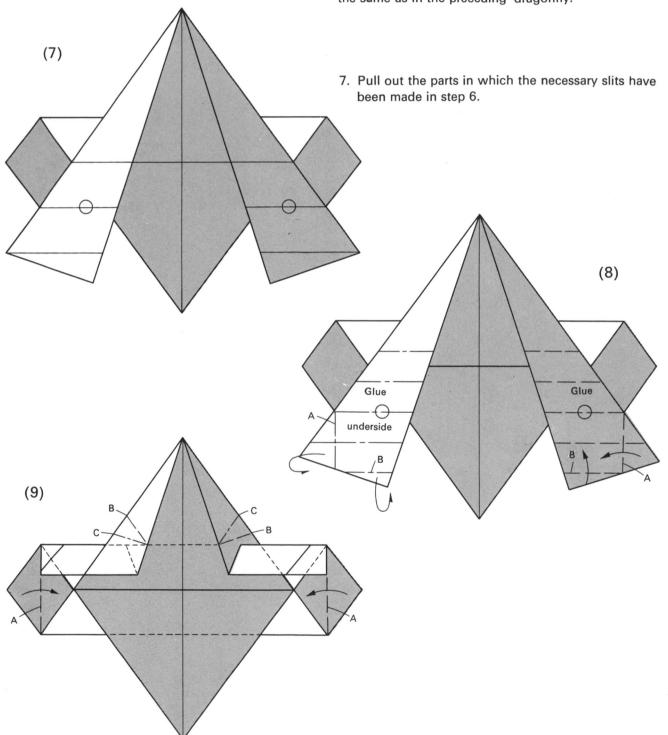

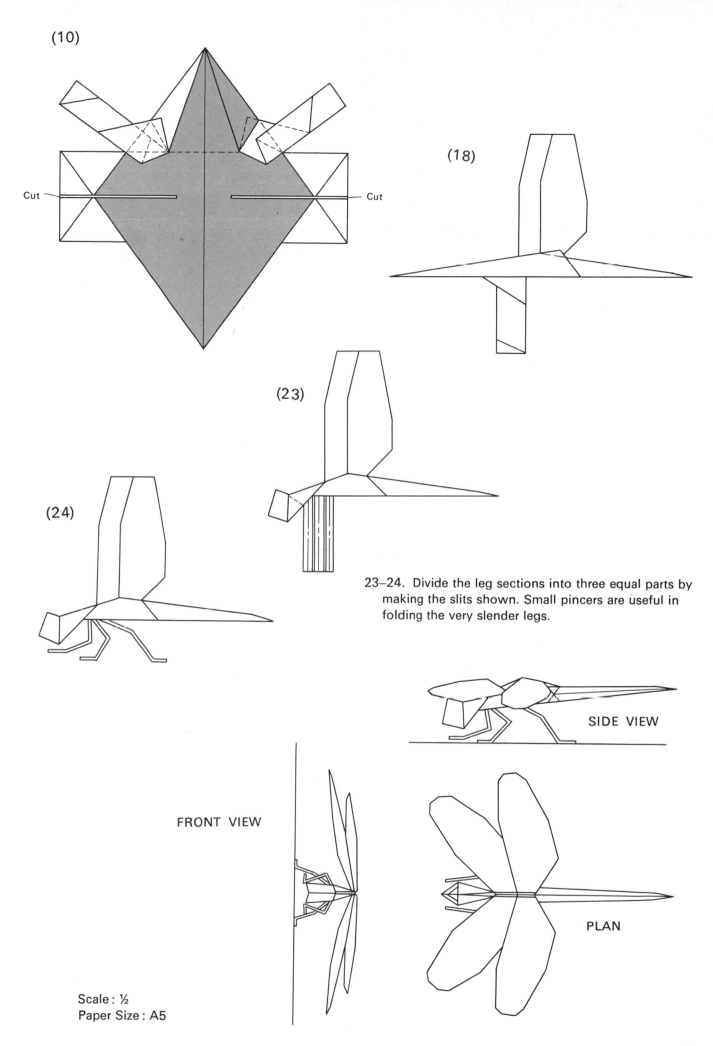

(10)

Cut

Cut

(18)

(23)

(24)

23–24. Divide the leg sections into three equal parts by making the slits shown. Small pincers are useful in folding the very slender legs.

SIDE VIEW

FRONT VIEW

PLAN

Scale: ½
Paper Size: A5

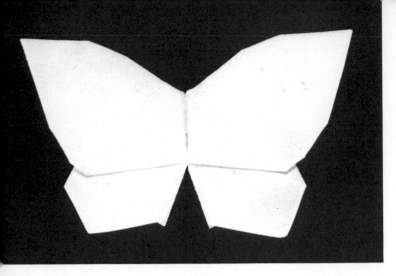

22. BUTTERFLY

The butterfly is a very popular subject of origami treatment, but in order to make one that glides well, the shape must be considerably simplified. This presents a surprising number of difficulties. Incidentally, though the butterfly's motion are slow and graceful, it is an extremely difficult creature to catch.

Sometimes the lovely insects seem to float as they glide gracefully downward on spring and summer days. This is the effect I have attempted to reproduce. In the model, the front wings are large and their forward incline is great. For this reason inevitably the center of gravity shifts rearward. This in turn makes it necessary to give the figure a marked upward angle. To prevent the center of gravity from shifting too far to the rear, I have weighted the head section.

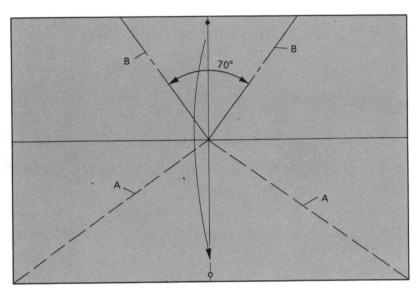

(1)

1. After establishing the center of the paper by folding it in half vertically and horizontally, make two valley folds on lines A. Next make the peak folds on lines B; you must use a protractor because lines B must be exactly 70° apart. Finally bring the black dot to the white dot.

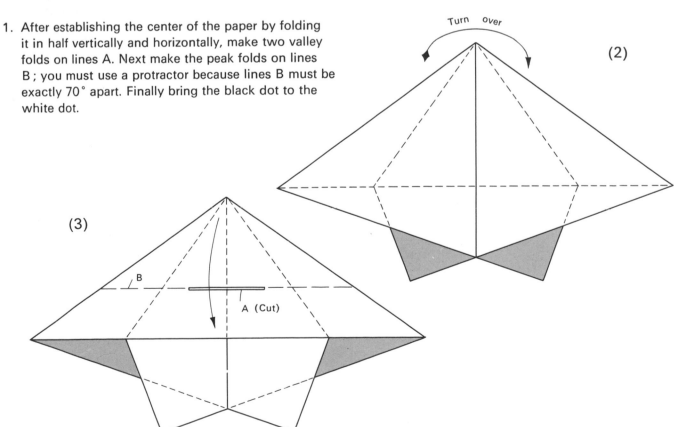

(2)

(3)

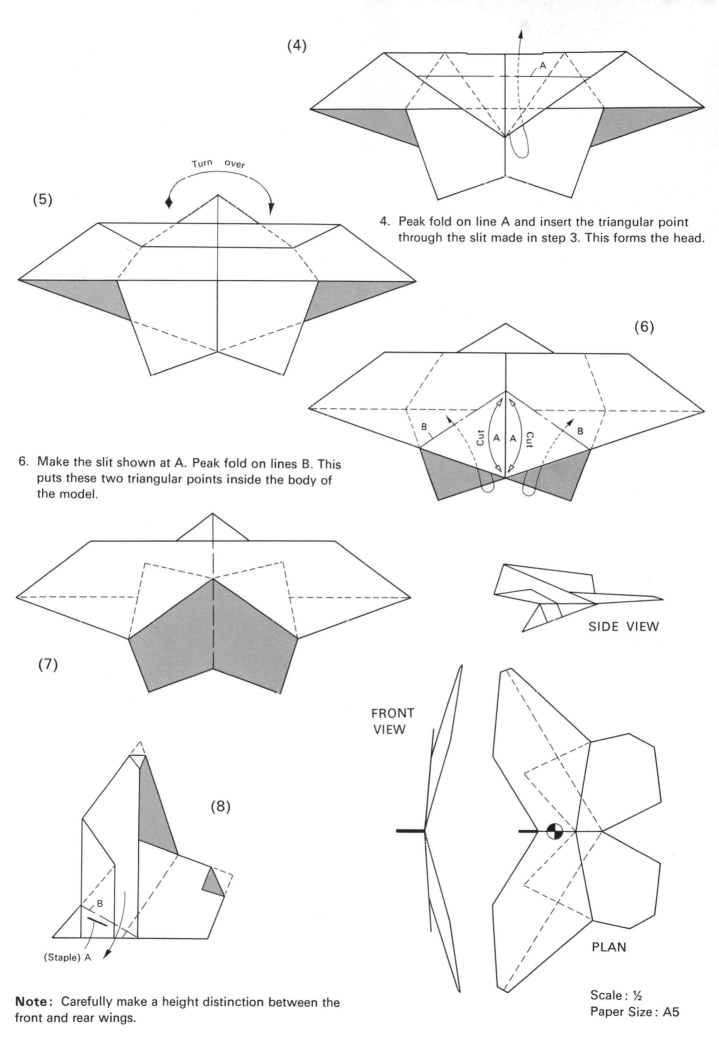

(4)

4. Peak fold on line A and insert the triangular point through the slit made in step 3. This forms the head.

(5)

Turn over

(6)

6. Make the slit shown at A. Peak fold on lines B. This puts these two triangular points inside the body of the model.

SIDE VIEW

(7)

FRONT VIEW

PLAN

(8)

(Staple) A

Note: Carefully make a height distinction between the front and rear wings.

Scale: ½
Paper Size: A5

23. MARSH HARRIER

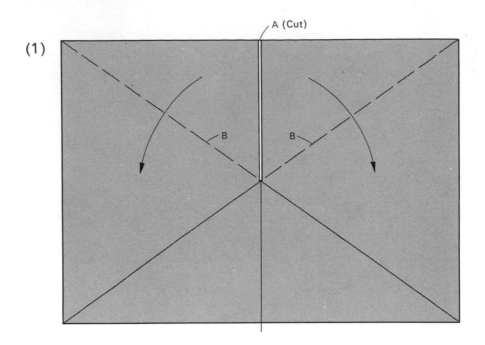

(1)

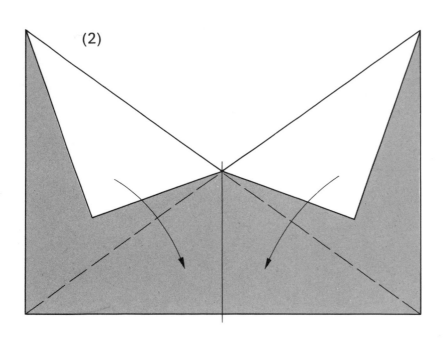

(4)

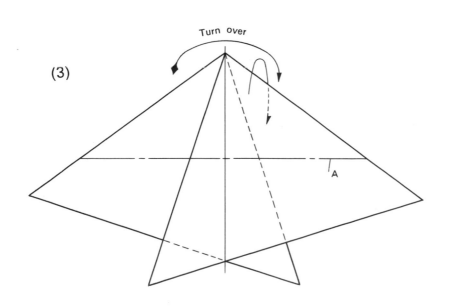

(2)

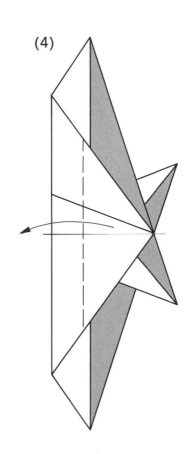

(3)

(5)

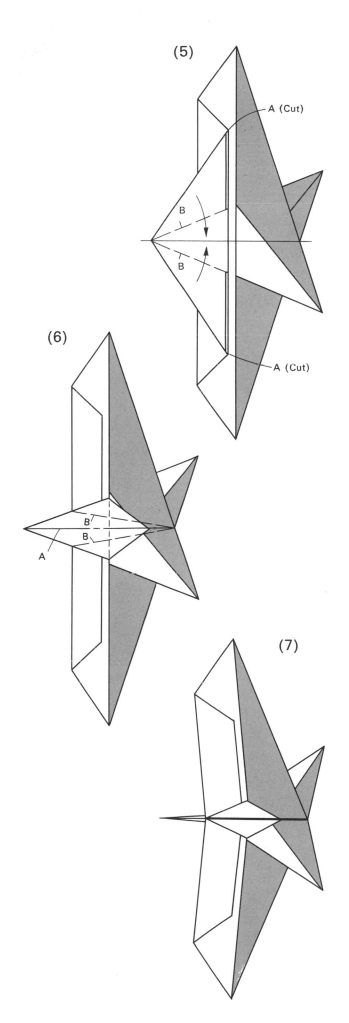

A (Cut)

B

B

A (Cut)

(6)

B'

B

A

(7)

This smaller member of the hawk and eagle family lives in the plains and swamps of Hokkaido, the northernmost of the Japanese islands. The sharply upturned wings assist the bird in soaring and gliding, its favorite mode of flight. Interestingly enough, to keep in good condition for its hunting raids, even when no prey is in the vicinity, the marsh harrier is said to practice by stooping and dropping on small stones or branches. Though the wings of the origami model are thicker than those of the true bird, in flight it very closely resembles the original. Do not be overly concerned that the right and left halves of the the tail are asymmetrical; it will not seriously affect the model's performance.

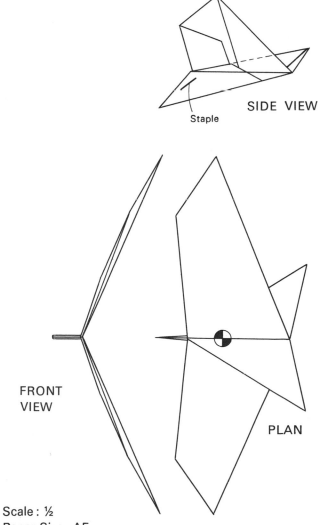

SIDE VIEW

Staple

FRONT VIEW

PLAN

Scale : ½
Paper Size : A5

24. BAT

In dealing with flying creatures it would be unfair to forget the one mammal that truly flies. The bat too is a frequent origami topic, but generally the aim is to produce an outline like that of the animal. Consequently there are many folds and winkled areas. For the sake of good flight performance, I have greatly simplified the shape.

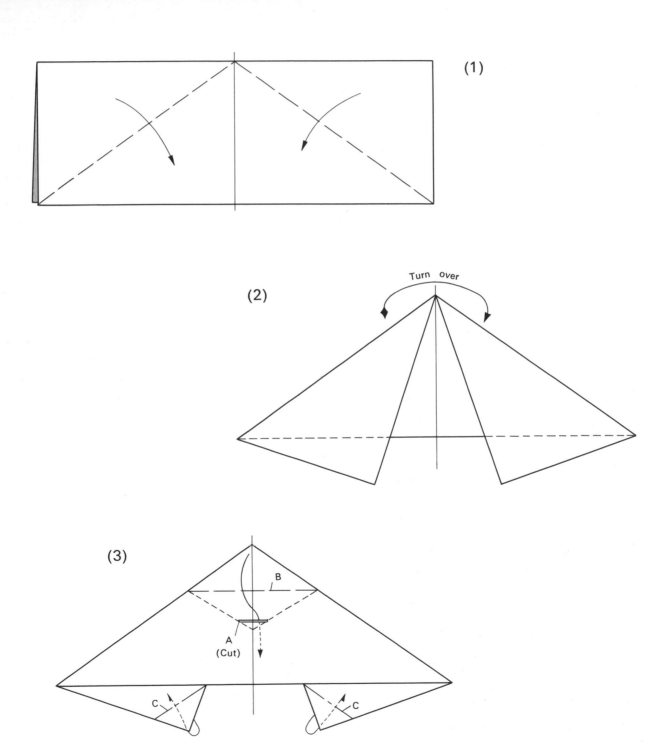

(1)

(2)

Turn over

(3)

B

A
(Cut)

C   C

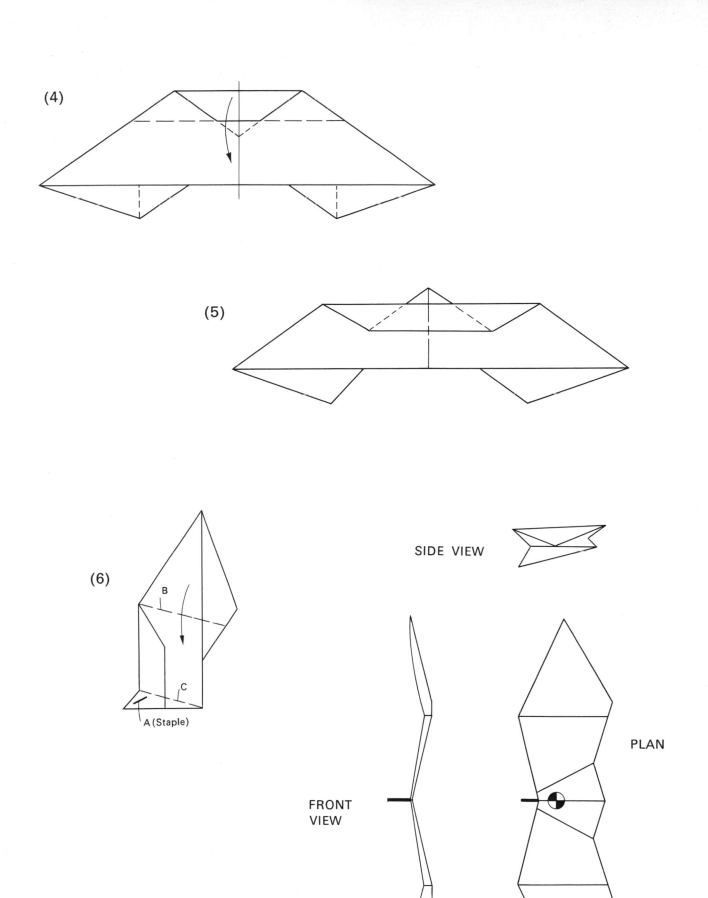

(4)

(5)

(6)

B

C

A (Staple)

SIDE VIEW

FRONT
VIEW

PLAN

Scale : ½
Paper Size : A5

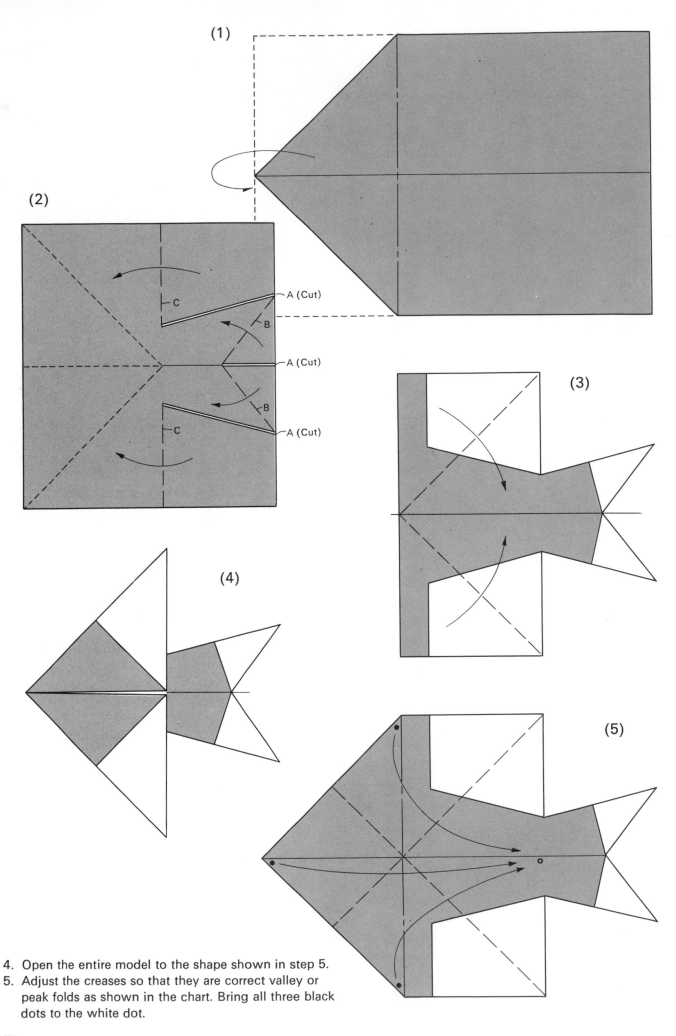

4. Open the entire model to the shape shown in step 5.
5. Adjust the creases so that they are correct valley or peak folds as shown in the chart. Bring all three black dots to the white dot.

25. SWALLOW (REVISED FLAT STYLE)

The improved version of the older flat-style swallow origami produces a model that flies like the real bird. The details of the head of this fold resulted from an examination of a Mexican paper-craft figure that a friend brought me as a souvenir. The folding method should be carefully learned because it is useful in number of different figures.

(6)

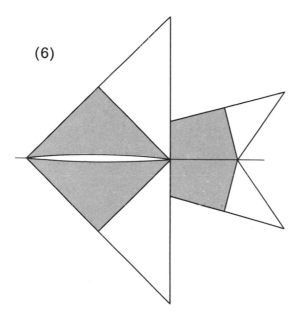

(7)

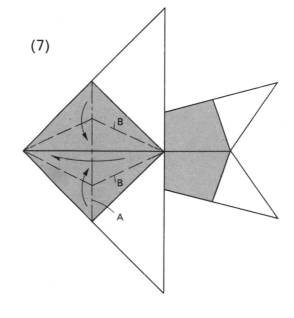

7. Make the creases in the square section of the head as indicated in the chart. Raise then crush the right and left sides by peak folding and folding around to the rear.

(8)

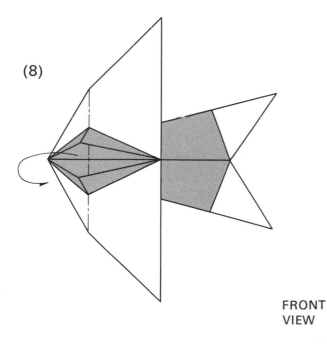

FRONT VIEW

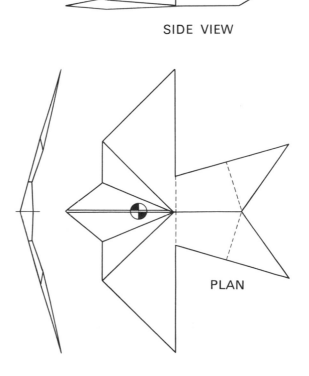

SIDE VIEW

PLAN

Scale: ½
Paper Size: A5

26. STORK

A completed model of the stork produces an origami that is both beautiful and a good flier. As photographs of the bird in flight show, it is elegant and powerful with its wings full spread and the pinions open like the fingers of a hand. Of course, the loveliness of the creature is enhanced by the charm of the legend that the stork brings babies.

BODY

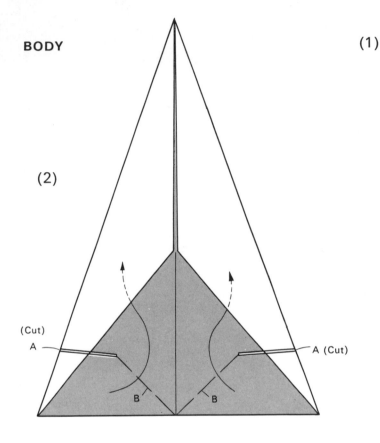

(2)

(Cut)

A

A (Cut)

B   B

(1)

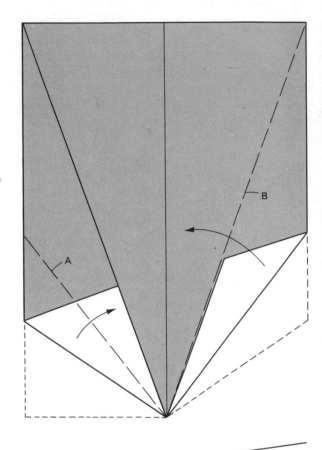

(5)

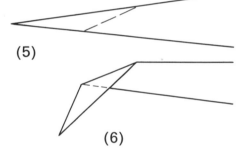

(6)

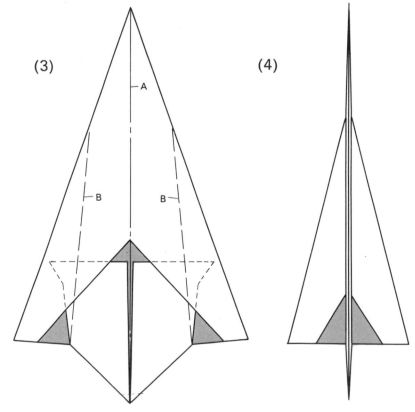

(3)

A

B   B

(4)

At this point I might give a brief explanation of the pinions and their function. In the case of square-tip wings, if the air current beneath them flows to the side and then rises to the wings upper surface, this current breaks up and creates a pressure differential that impedes lift power. (In aircraft this is called wingtip stalling.) Since this phenomenon occurs at the rear triangular corners of the tips, in order to prevent it, the tip corners may be trimmed off to form oval-tip wings. Or the ends of the wings may be outfitted with a row of slender feathers, which are called pinions. Since oval-end wings inevitably require large surface areas, the wings of big birds that fly in somewhat cramped forest spaces are more functionally efficient if they are short and broad; consequently, in their cases pinions are better than oval-end wings.

WINGS

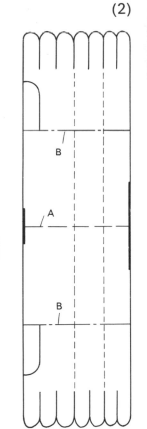

(1)

Glue underside

Turn over

(2)

B

A

B

Pinions are used most in slow flying and landing. At such times, their heights are adjusted to be lower in front and to rise gradually toward the rear of the wings. Air flowing past the front pinions, forces a current to move over the upper surfaces of the next rows of pinions and in this way improves lift.

Now you have a general idea of the necessity and function of the pinions. Although it flies, this model is very realistic even when suspended on a string.

WINGS

1. Fold the paper lengthwise to make a small margin on the right. Glue these two layers together then valley fold as shown.
2. Peak fold on the center line. Peak fold on lines B ; also cut the small feathers on the leading edge. Cut and trim the pinions as shown in the chart ; they should all be of equal width. Put glue on the wings in a strip as wide as the body. Attach the wings to the body and adjust the heights of the pinions as indicated.

PINIONS

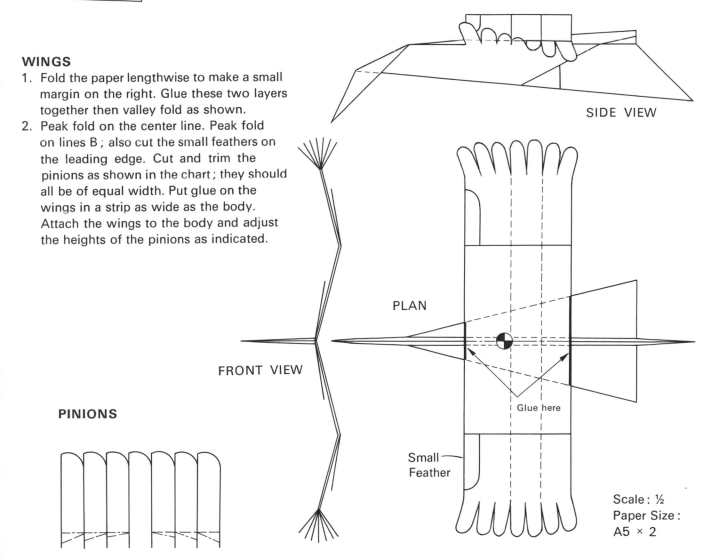

SIDE VIEW

PLAN

FRONT VIEW

Glue here

Small Feather

Scale : ½
Paper Size :
A5 × 2

27. FLYING CRANE

Like the stork, the crane is a large handsome bird. It is widely distributed throughout Asia, North America, and other parts of the northern hemisphere. Unlike the stork, however, the crane does not light in trees but spends its time either in the air or on the surface of the earth. When flying it is one of the most graceful of all birds. This origami expresses the crane in flight. The method of making the wings differs from that of other origami birds in that the paper is not sharply creased. The aim is to give the wings a curved cross section. Resembling what are called thick wings in aviation, this structure makes possible direct unmannered flight. As in the case of the stork, the crane origami is made in two parts: wings and body.

(1)

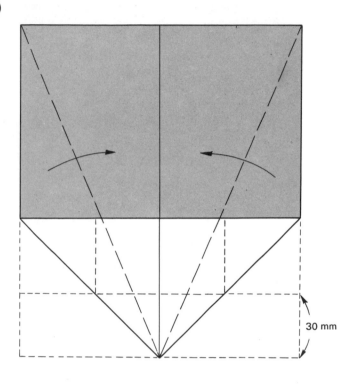

BODY

(2)

30 mm

(3)

2. Make the incisions shown. Valley fold on lines B and insert the flaps under the lower folded section.

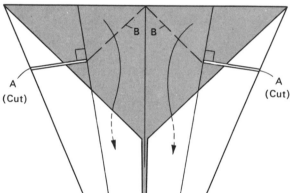

WINGS

(2)

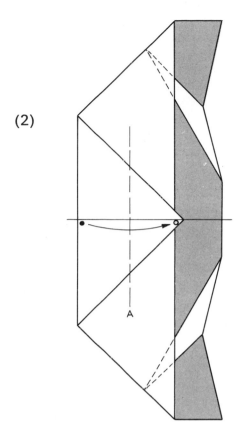

(1)

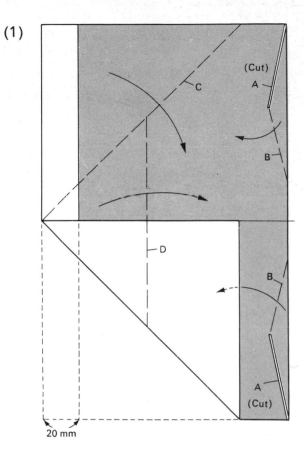

20 mm

2. Glue the triangular flap in place. Valley fold on line A. But notice that this line does not extend to the ends of the wings; in other words, the crease must be made only in that area that will be close to the body in the finished crane.

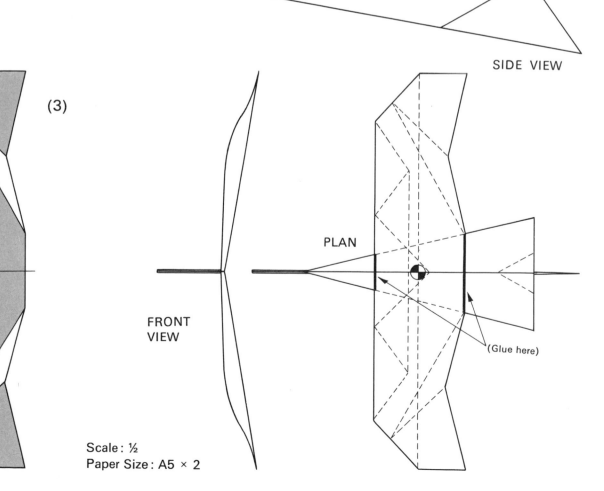

(3)

FRONT
VIEW

SIDE VIEW

PLAN

(Glue here)

Scale: ½
Paper Size: A5 × 2

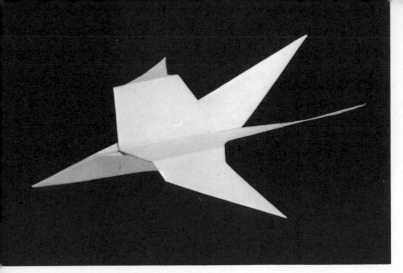

28. FLYING SWALLOW

This is another version of the bird that appears on p. 56. The clean lines and slender figure of the swallow flying among the houses and buildings of towns have long made it a popular subject for origami. I made origami figures and cutout planes based on this bird when I was a child, but combining an accurate approximation of its appearance and a simulation of its action in flight is difficult. For that reason it made me very happy when at the First International Paper Airplane Competition held in San Francisco, my swallow plane won first prize. You will find the speed and the acrobatic flying of the origami swallow a source of great amusement and pleasure. Be very careful when flying it however. The sharp pointed nose could seriously damage a person's eyes.

(1)

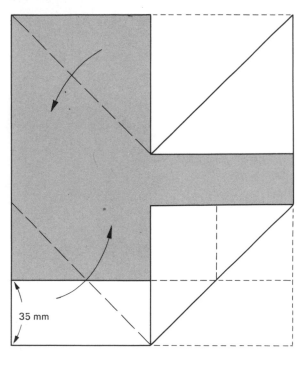

35 mm

BODY

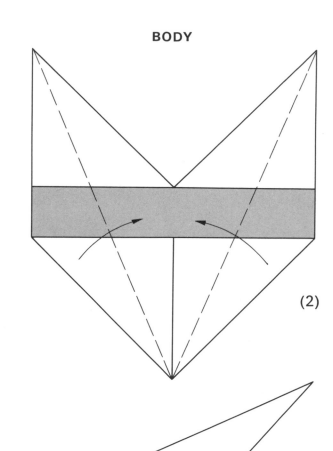

(2)

(4)

(3)

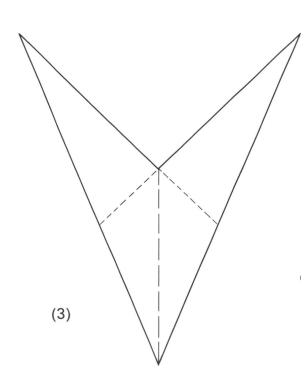

(5)

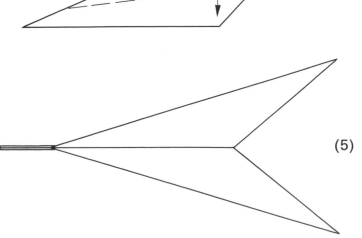

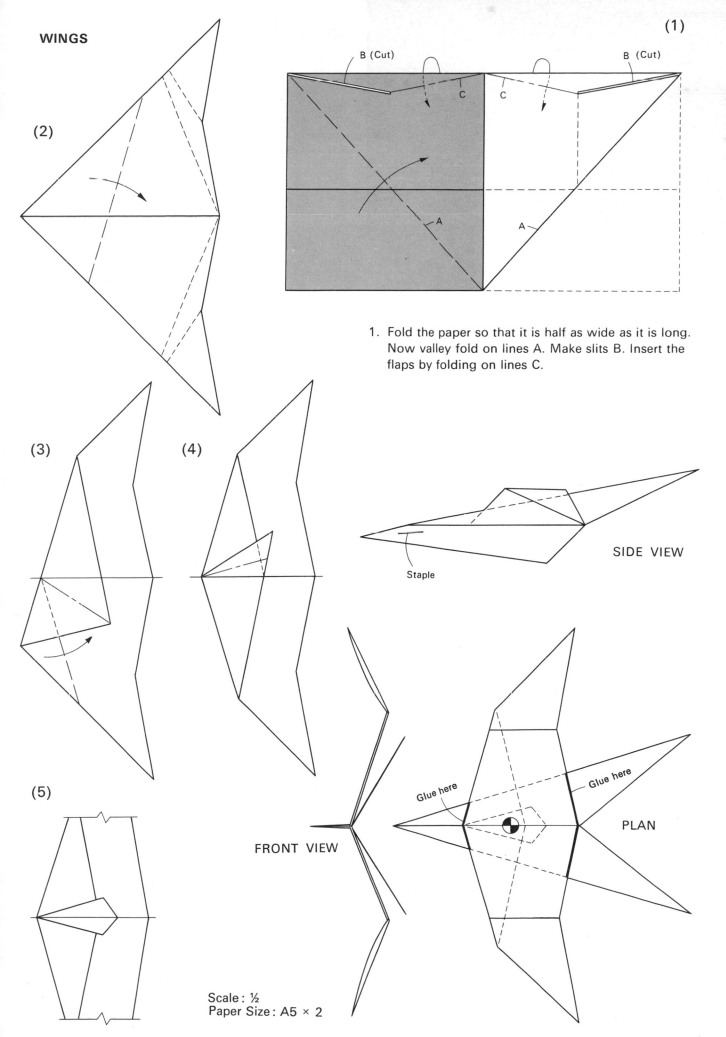

WINGS

(1)

B (Cut)   C   C   B (Cut)

A   A

(2)

1. Fold the paper so that it is half as wide as it is long. Now valley fold on lines A. Make slits B. Insert the flaps by folding on lines C.

(3)   (4)

SIDE VIEW

Staple

(5)

FRONT VIEW

Glue here   Glue here

PLAN

Scale: ½
Paper Size: A5 × 2